FAITHFUL SERVANT OF GOD

Stephen J. Lennox

Copyright © 2016 by Stephen J. Lennox
Published by Wesleyan Publishing House
Indianapolis, Indiana 46250
Printed in the United States of America
ISBN: 978-0-89827-906-1
ISBN (e-book): 978-0-89827-907-8

Library of Congress Cataloging-in-Publication Data

Lennox, Stephen J.
  Moses : faithful servant of God / Stephen J. Lennox.
     pages cm
  Includes bibliographical references.
  ISBN 978-0-89827-906-1 (pbk.)
  1. Moses (Biblical leader)--Biblical teaching. I. Title.
  BS580.M6L46 2016
  222'.1092--dc23
                          2015026175

All Scripture quotations, unless otherwise indicated, are taken from the Holy Bible, New International Version®, NIV ®. Copyright ©1973, 1978, 1984, 2011 by Biblica, Inc. Used by permission of Zondervan. All rights reserved worldwide. www.zondervan.com. The "NIV" and "New International Version" are trademarks registered in the United States Patent and Trademark Office by Biblica, Inc.

Scripture quotations marked (ESV) are from The Holy Bible, English Standard Version® (ESV®), copyright © 2001 by Crossway, a publishing ministry of Good News Publishers. Used by permission. All rights reserved.

Scripture quotations marked (NASB) are taken from the *New American Standard Bible*®, Copyright © 1960, 1962, 1963, 1968, 1971, 1972, 1973, 1975, 1977, 1995 by The Lockman Foundation. Used by permission.

Excerpts marked (NJB) are from *The New Jerusalem Bible*, copyright © 1985 by Darton, Longman & Todd, Ltd. and Doubleday & Company, Inc. Reprinted by permission.

Scripture quotations marked (ASV) are taken from the *American Standard Version*. Public domain.

Scripture quotations marked (NLT) are taken from the Holy Bible, New Living Translation, copyright © 1996, 2004, 2007, 2013 by Tyndale House Foundation. Used by permission of Tyndale House Publishers, Inc., Carol Stream, Illinois 60188. All rights reserved.

Scripture quotations marked (NRSV) are from the *New Revised Standard Version Bible*, copyright © 1989 National Council of the Churches of Christ in the United States of America. Used by permission. All rights reserved.

Scripture quotations marked (KJV) are taken from THE HOLY BIBLE, KING JAMES VERSION.

All rights reserved. No part of this publication may be reproduced, stored in a retrieval system, or transmitted in any form or by any means—electronic, mechanical, photocopy, recording, or any other—except for brief quotations in printed reviews, without the prior written permission of the publisher.

To my parents, Ian and Charmaine Lennox,
who have modeled lifetime service to God's people.

Contents

Acknowledgements	7
Introduction	9
1. Preparing the Faithful Servant	19
2. Calling the Faithful Servant, Part 1	35
3. Calling the Faithful Servant, Part 2	49
4. Divine-Human Synergy	63
5. The Way God Works	77
6. Moses and the Passover	89
7. The Servant in the Wilderness	105
8. The Faithful Servant and the Liberating Law, Part 1	121
9. The Faithful Servant and the Liberating Law, Part 2	137
10. Moses under Fire	155
11. Faithful to the End: Moses and the New Generation	173
Notes	191

Acknowledgements

I'm grateful to Rachael Stevenson and the editorial team at Wesleyan Publishing House for the invitation to write this book and their assistance in bringing the concept to fruition. I also appreciate all the students I've taught through the years who have helped me better understand Moses. To my colleagues at Indiana Wesleyan University and Kingswood University who have taught me what it means to serve others, thank you.

I want to especially thank my wife, Eileen, for her love and support through all our adventures. Finally, my gratitude to God, who has called me to a ministry of studying and sharing God's Word, knows no bounds.

Introduction

In the opening chapters of the book of Hebrews, the author developed his theme of Jesus' superiority over all forms of revelation that had come before. The writer began by showing how Christ is greater than the angels. Then in chapter 3, the author turned his attention to Moses.

> Therefore, holy brothers and sisters, who share in the heavenly calling, fix your thoughts on Jesus, whom we acknowledge as our apostle and high priest. He was faithful to the one who appointed him, just as Moses was faithful in all God's house. Jesus has been found worthy of greater honor than Moses, just as the builder of a house has greater honor than the house itself. For every house is built by someone, but God is the builder of everything. "Moses was faithful as a servant in all God's house," bearing witness to what would be spoken by God in the future. But Christ is faithful as the Son over God's house. And we are his house, if indeed we hold firmly

to our confidence and the hope in which we glory. (Heb. 3:1–6)

In verse 5, we meet the descriptive phrase that will serve as the focal point for this book: "Moses was faithful as a servant in all God's house."

A SERVANT

The writer of Hebrews identified Moses' role as that of a servant to highlight the contrast between a servant in the house and the builder of the house (3:3), and between the servant in the household and the son who owns the household (v. 6). Although Moses and Jesus were both God's servants (v. 2), Jesus is greater than Moses for he has built the house that is God's church, and he is the son and heir of the Master, God himself.

As great as Moses was, Christ is greater. Moses was an instrumental part of that house—like its foundation and walls—but Christ is the builder of the house. Moses had seen God in the burning bush and on Mount Sinai, but Jesus is God, "the radiance of God's glory and the exact representation of his being, sustaining all things by his powerful word" (1:3). Moses received the law on Sinai and transmitted it to the people, but Jesus fulfilled the law, both perfectly obeying it and superseding it. As Gareth Cockerill has written, "Moses bore witness to what God would reveal through his Son."[1] Moses established the Old Testament priesthood, ordaining the first priests and instructing them in their duties, but Jesus came as the great High Priest who resolved the issue of sin once for all time in his own sacrifice. Because Jesus lives forever, he has a permanent priesthood enabling him:

INTRODUCTION

Therefore he is able to save completely those who come to God through him, because he always lives to intercede for them. Such a high priest truly meets our need—one who is holy, blameless, pure, set apart from sinners, exalted above the heavens. Unlike the other high priests, he does not need to offer sacrifices day after day, first for his own sins, and then for the sins of the people. He sacrificed for their sins once for all when he offered himself. For the law appoints as high priests men in all their weakness; but the oath, which came after the law, appointed the Son, who has been made perfect forever. (7:25–28)

The author of Hebrews summarized his point: "We do have such a high priest, who sat down at the right hand of the throne of the Majesty in heaven, and who serves in the sanctuary, the true tabernacle set up by the Lord, not by a mere human being" (Heb. 8:1–2). The priesthood established by Moses is fulfilled and surpassed by the priestly work of Christ.

The apostle Paul went one step beyond the author of Hebrews, though in a direction wholly in line with the understanding of the latter. Paul identified Moses as an Old Testament model or pattern of Jesus. We might call Moses a "type" of Christ, typifying aspects of the Lord's character and actions that would be more fully revealed in the incarnation. Paul revealed this thinking in writing to the church at Corinth: "For I do not want you to be ignorant of the fact, brothers and sisters, that our ancestors were all under the cloud and that they all passed through the sea. They were all baptized into Moses in the cloud and in the sea. They all ate the same spiritual food and drank the same spiritual drink; for they drank from the spiritual rock that accompanied them, and that rock was Christ" (1 Cor. 10:1–4).

The nineteenth-century divine Andrew Murray drew out the correlations between Moses and Christ: both suffered at the hands of their fellow Israelites and were rejected by them; both exercised great zeal and sacrificed greatly for God; both interceded on behalf of others; both enjoyed unparalleled fellowship with God; and both offered their lives for God's people—God declined Moses' offer but accepted that of Jesus.[2] "As the one who led God's people through the wilderness toward the Promised Land," observes Cockerill, "Moses foreshadowed the Son as our pioneer who brings us into the heavenly homeland."[3]

IN GOD'S HOUSE

What does the writer of Hebrews mean by the phrase "God's house" (3:5)? This term is not original with this writer but is a paraphrase of Numbers 12:7, where God spoke of Moses as "faithful in all my house." In fact, this entire passage from Hebrews 3 relies heavily on Numbers 12:6–8. The house to which God referred in the Numbers passage is not a physical structure but a household with himself as the head, the Israelites as God's servants (see Lev. 25:42), and Moses as the chief servant appointed to manage it. While it would also be correct to speak of Moses and the Israelites as God's children, the master-servant analogy is used more often throughout the opening books of the Old Testament.

Moses' appointment as servant had taken place at the burning bush (Ex. 4:10). Although initially reluctant, Moses accepted the challenge and grew into the role. The Israelites were reluctant to accept his leadership but seem to have done so after crossing the Red Sea (Ex. 14:31). Even so, they challenged his leadership many times and tested his patience many more times before his service ended and that responsibility passed to Joshua.

INTRODUCTION

All of this—the appointment of Moses, the deliverance of the Israelites, the travel through the wilderness, the preparation for crossing into Canaan—was part of God's redemptive plan. God began this plan with Abraham, calling him from Mesopotamia and making a covenant with him. In this covenant, God promised to make Abraham into a great nation and bless all other nations through him. Much of Genesis describes the slow outworking of God's plan as this elderly couple produced a son, who in turn produced two sons. One of these, Jacob, became the father of a dozen sons. By the end of Genesis, the descendants of Abraham and Sarah numbered seventy, and they lived in Egypt.

When the suffering of Abraham's descendants in Egypt became severe, God appointed his servant Moses to lead the rest of his servants out of Egypt and into Canaan. On the way, they received the law on Mount Sinai. This law explained how those in God's household must live with each other and with those in the community and how they must honor their Master in worship. Through the law, God was reshaping their identity: no longer were they Egyptian slaves; now they were servants of Yahweh, the living God. Their journey to Canaan, which would ordinarily have taken less than a fortnight, lasted forty years due to their rebellion. The members of God's household wandered for four decades until he determined they could enter the Promised Land. Moses would lead them to the land and would see it from Mount Nebo, but he would not enter. A new head servant, Joshua, would take his place. Moses' work was a matter of "bearing witness to what would be spoken by God in the future" (Heb. 3:5), that being the unfolding of God's redemptive plan.

God's plan called for the Israelites to conquer Canaan, establish a kingdom, build a temple, and become a guiding light for other nations. However, God's servants stumbled due to a lack of faith, just as they had done in the desert. But God remained faithful, restoring them as a nation and bringing forth the Messiah from that nation. Through the life, death, and resurrection of Jesus, God's plan was consummated. The church—a continuation of the earlier household but now expanded to include Gentiles—was given the responsibility to carry out God's work in the world, guided and equipped by God's Spirit. Much of the New Testament describes the beginning of this expansion and anticipates its final expression in the book of Revelation. One of the closing scenes in that final book describes a great and marvelous sign, the victorious servants of God standing beside the sea, holding harps given to them by God. They "sang the song of God's servant Moses and of the Lamb" (Rev. 15:3), a single song written about two faithful servants in God's house.

A FAITHFUL SERVANT

Moses' story is just one part—though a very important part—of the story of God's redemptive plan unfolded among humanity. Moses is not the main character, even in his own story; that role belongs to God. There is, however, a long tradition of seeing Moses and other Old Testament characters as examples to follow. Hebrews 11 contains a well-known example of this, what some call the Hall of the Heroes of Faith. Although our circumstances may differ from the biblical heroes catalogued there, we learn much from them, especially Moses.

The Bible was not written primarily to provide instructions for how to be a faithful servant in God's house, yet we glean important life principles from its pages. We serve the same God as did those original servants, and his character does not change. We are all called to be God's servants (see 2 Tim. 2:24; 3:17; Rev. 19:10); some are

INTRODUCTION

even called, like Moses, to serve by leading other servants (see Eph. 3:7; 6:21). It stands to reason that by observing how Moses prepared for his role, how he served, what challenges he faced, how he was punished, and how he prepared the people for a transition to a new leader, we can understand something of what it means for us to become faithful servants in God's house.

Some of these lessons are apparent in Hebrews 3. First, we see that God's servant is not self-appointed; no one applies for this job. God appoints faithful servants, even as he appointed Christ to his role (v. 2). In the opening three chapters of this book, we will look closely at how Moses was prepared for his role and then called at the burning bush.

Next in Hebrews 3, we note that God's servant participates with God in his work; the servant is not self-employed. Moses' specific role was "bearing witness to what would be spoken by God in the future" (v. 5). In other words, the message was God's not Moses'. Moses did not originate this plan but accepted his role in it and faithfully executed the work assigned. So it is with all faithful servants: They are busy about their Master's business. In five chapters of this book, we will observe Moses doing God's business, leading the Israelites out of Egypt and through the wilderness. We will consider how he served under pressure and how he continued to serve God up to the very end of his life.

Third, we see that God's servant receives both the great blessing of encountering God and the great responsibility of passing along what he has learned to others. Moses met with God more than once, initially at the burning bush but more intensively at Mount Sinai. His relationship with God was so close that God described them as relating face-to-face (more literally, "mouth to mouth"), enabling Moses to understand God "clearly and not in riddles" (Num. 12:8). While this degree of closeness may have been unique to Moses among God's servants, each of us has the privilege of encountering God.

These encounters bring great blessing but the purpose is to equip us to better serve him by making him known to others. Moses did this when he told the Israelites God had met with him at a burning bush and wanted to set them free from slavery and when he passed along God's instructions regarding Passover. However, the most significant instance of Moses encountering God and sharing the fruit of that experience took place at Mount Sinai. There God inscribed his revelation on tablets of stone, and Moses carried them down to the people to explain in detail what God had commanded. Through the written law, God revealed a clearer picture of the moral law written on the heart of every person. He used the law to turn a large group of slaves into a nation he could use to further his plan. The nature and purpose of this law and Moses' role in its reception and distribution are the focus of two chapters of this book.

Moses is a wonderful example of a faithful servant because he executed his responsibilities to the good of the people and, more importantly, to the glory of God. Moses put the needs of others above his own. We see this in his willingness to leave the safety of his life tending sheep to shepherd God's people. It is apparent in his begging God to pardon the Israelites, even after God promised to make Moses the new Abraham. We see Moses putting others ahead of himself when he appealed for his sister, even after she rebelled against his authority. And Moses was faithful when it was necessary to correct the Israelites in order to instruct them.

Moses' faithfulness to the people for God was an act of faithfulness to God. God's honor was uppermost in Moses' mind. When Pharaoh refused to allow the people to go free, Moses grew "hot with anger" (Ex. 11:8) at how the king was dishonoring the King of Kings. When God threatened to destroy the Israelites, Moses

INTRODUCTION

reminded him that it would reflect negatively on Yahweh's honor. There was, however, one occasion when Moses failed to honor God above himself, a mistake for which Moses paid dearly. This exception only proves the rule: The faithful servant must honor God.

Given Moses' faithfulness, it is no surprise that God showed full confidence in him. He allowed Moses to speak for him to Pharaoh, he worked miracles through his servant, and he allowed Moses to be honored by the Egyptians. More than once God changed his plans in response to Moses' intercession. Yahweh defended Moses against all challenges to his authority and buried Moses with his own hands. Because Moses was faithful to God, God was faithful to Moses. Indeed, "no one has ever shown the mighty power or performed the awesome deeds that Moses did in the sight of all Israel" (Deut. 34:12).

CONCLUSION

Through the pages of this book, we will take a closer look at Moses, faithful servant in all God's house and at the Master he faithfully served. Our study begins with events prior to Moses' birth, then turns to his miraculous preservation as an infant and his upbringing in Pharaoh's court. We consider his failure as a savior and his flight from Egypt, then his call at the burning bush and his role in the exodus. We follow Moses and the Israelites through the wilderness, observing his development as a servant through the challenges he faced up to his final days.

Through our study, we seek to learn more about the character of the Master and the nature of faithful service so that we, too, can be faithful servants of God. Faithfulness to God, after all, "is the spirit of God's house, the mark of being of his household. It was so with Moses the servant. It was so with Christ the Son. It must be so through the whole household. Be it so with us: Faithful to God."[4]

1

Preparing the Faithful Servant

Exodus 1–2

The story of Moses begins well before his birth. For decades prior, forces had been at work that would shape Moses into a faithful servant, forces directed by a sovereign hand—God's, not Pharaoh's. The first two chapters of Exodus recount the Egyptian oppression of the Israelites and the beginning of God's plan to deliver his people. By the end of these chapters, God's servant would be prepared to enter God's service, although the path to preparation was far from what we might have expected.

TRANSITION FROM GENESIS TO EXODUS

To set the stage for what God would do through Moses, the narrator of Exodus began the story well before Moses' birth and miraculous preservation as an infant. He began with the sons of Jacob who came from famine-ravaged Canaan to find relief in Egypt. The narrator listed these sons according to their mothers, beginning with the sons of Leah, then Rachel, Bilhah (Rachel's maid), and Zilpah (Leah's maid). He mentioned Joseph last because he was already in Egypt, thanks to his brothers (Ex. 1:5).

We learn that Joseph, his brothers, and all that generation had died, since as many as four centuries had passed (see Ex. 12:40–41; Gen. 15:13, 16). By this time the Israelites had multiplied greatly. Exodus 1:7 describes that growth using five verbs and two adverbs: "were fruitful . . . increased abundantly . . . multiplied . . . waxed exceeding mighty . . . the land was filled with them" (KJV). By emphasizing their growth, the narrator demonstrated that God was fulfilling his promise to make a great nation out of Abraham's descendants (see Gen. 12:2). The narrator also anticipated the looming conflict with their host nation, Egypt.

EGYPTIAN OPPRESSION OF THE ISRAELITES

The narrator next described how the conflict began. A new king had come to Egypt's throne, one who did not know about Joseph (Ex. 1:8). Although it is possible that the Egyptians literally forgot about Joseph, this seems unlikely given his status as a high-ranking official in their government and their penchant for keeping careful records. More likely, the phrase refers to this pharaoh's decision not to acknowledge Joseph's role in preserving Egypt, now that the Israelites had become a threat. Such ingratitude is more understandable given that Joseph was not a native-born Egyptian, and xenophobic attitudes ran deep in Egyptian history. The narrator did not mention the name of this pharaoh. However, if we accept an early date for the exodus, it would likely be the founder of the Eighteenth

Dynasty, Ahmose (1552–1556 BC), while a later date makes Seti I (Sethos I) (1294–1279 BC) of the Nineteenth Dynasty the likely candidate.

Egyptian fear of the Israelites arose for several reasons. The Egyptians were already suspicious of foreigners and had only recently broken free from decades under foreign rulers. Israel appeared to be a growing internal threat. Should another nation threaten Egypt, Israel could align themselves with the invaders and turn on their hosts, defeating the Egyptians. The Egyptian fear that the Israelites would "leave the country" (1:10) does not refer to a fear of lost slave labor, since they had not yet enslaved the Israelites. They were afraid the Israelites would decimate and plunder them, and then depart the country, the Egyptians being too weak to stop them. Perhaps the greatest source of Egyptian fear was the remarkable reproductive rate of the Israelites, suggesting the favor of Israel's God. Such supernatural support called for Egypt to "deal shrewdly with them" (v. 10), that is, with wisdom.

Egyptian Plan A involved forcing the Israelites to work on several large-scale building projects (vv. 11–12). To this the Egyptians added the indignity of forcing the Israelites to build storage cities in the very country their ancestor, Joseph, had been instrumental in saving through a system of grain storage. The Egyptian plan failed, however, for the harder they worked the Israelites the more they reproduced. Two terms are reused in 1:12 that appeared in the initial description of Israel's population growth in verse 7: *multiplied* and *spread*. The Egyptians' dread of the Israelites signals their conclusion that this growth was divinely produced. And this dread is a more serious reaction than before, something closer to "horrified" or "alarmed."

So the Egyptians implemented Plan B, stepping up their oppression of the Israelites (vv. 13–14). The word *ruthlessly* appears twice in these verses and captures the essence of this plan. They subjected the Israelites, more literally, to "toil that breaks." This hard labor was just what God had predicted (see Gen. 15:13), and its bitterness would be remembered later through the bitter herbs of the Passover meal (Ex. 12:8).

Although no mention is made of the outcome of Plan B, its failure is implied in the execution of the still more desperate Plan C (1:15–21). Now Pharaoh commanded the Hebrew midwives to kill all male babies born to the Israelites, allowing only female babies to live. They were probably told to do this secretly, before anyone knew whether the infant was stillborn or alive. There must have been more midwives than just these two, who are likely mentioned as heads of a guild. (Note the reference to other midwives in v. 19). Pharaoh instructed them to observe the gender of the newborn and then kill the males, but the midwives feared God instead.

When Pharaoh challenged the midwives for failing to carry out his commands, they lied. Some scholars fault these women for their deception even while applauding their obedience to God. Others point out that truth telling in the ancient world may have had more to do with loyalty to one's god than strict adherence to the facts. God oversight of the midwives' deceit can be seen in two ways. First, God allowed them to establish homes and families. Aside from the joy of having their own children, such a blessing demonstrates God's intention to give the Israelites a future. Second, God allowed the narrator to reveal their names while the pharaoh who threatened them remains anonymous. Naming a figure or leaving a figure unnamed were literary devices practiced in the ancient Near East to show honor or disgrace respectively. Thanks to the faithful midwives, Plan C fails as well (v. 20). This brings the desperate pharaoh to Plan D, authorization for all Egyptians to kill all male Hebrew babies (v. 22).

God was not absent from this chapter, though the circumstances seem to indicate otherwise. His people were suffering, oppressed by the Egyptians who had forgotten the debt of gratitude owed to Joseph and were apparently forgotten by the God who had promised to bless them. Their situation grew continually more difficult, escalating from forced labor to infanticide.

Yet we see God at work. He is ultimately responsible for the remarkable population growth among the Israelites, a growth rate the Egyptians were powerless to slow. Even they recognize that something awe inspiring, perhaps even dreadful, was at work. We see God's blessing in the favor shown to the faithful midwives, Shiphrah and Puah. God's attention to these relatively obscure individuals conveys to the reader that God's watchful eye was on this whole situation.

If God was watching, why wasn't he working on behalf of his people? He was by allowing Israel time to develop from a family into a nation capable of occupying the Promised Land of Canaan. The hardships themselves are further evidence of God's work. Israel's deliverance was approaching, but how many would be willing to leave Egypt, the only land they had known for generations, to go to another, currently occupied by powerful nations? Few indeed, unless life in Egypt was unbearable. And the Israelites were not the only ones shaped by these experiences. The Egyptians were beginning to see their long-term guests in a different light. No longer could they view them as ignorant, odd, immigrant peasants— not after recognizing something supernaturally at work in them. Eventually, this recognition, reinforced by the ten plagues, persuaded the Egyptians that the Israelites had to go. So the process of extricating the Israelites from Egypt began well before the plagues with the very hardships described in the first chapter of Exodus.

God was at work in another way as well: raising up Moses. Beginning with Exodus 2, the narrator shifted his attention from the nation's troubles to the man called by God to deliver his people from their troubles.

THE BIRTH AND EARLY LIFE OF MOSES

Exodus 2 is a carefully crafted piece of literature. It begins and ends with a marriage and the birth of a son. At the end of the first and third minor sections, this son is named and his name is explained. Throughout the chapter are repeated references to daughters. The first chapter of Exodus transitions smoothly to the second: Pharaoh's grave command is the backdrop that prompts Moses' mother to take the drastic step of placing her son in the crocodile-infested waters of the Nile River.

The opening ten verses of Exodus 2 describe Moses' birth and rescue. Although well-known to even the youngest student in Sunday school, this story gives rise to many questions and surprises. One question is why God chose to bring Israel's deliverer from the tribe of Levi (2:1) rather than one of the other tribes. Both Moses' mother and father were Levites. One commentator rightly suggests that this is meant to highlight Moses' priestly, intercessory role on Israel's behalf.[1] Another reason may be the prominence of the tabernacle and sacrificial system in the law Moses would receive on Mount Sinai, a system in which the tribe of Levi would play a central role.

Another question concerns the meaning of Moses' mother's statement that "he was a fine child" (v. 2). The Hebrew word for *fine* is "good" and could have any number of meanings. The author of Hebrews suggests "good" here means handsome or beautiful (11:23 ESV). In the ancient world, as in our own, one's physical appearance was understood to have a bearing on one's success in life. The NIV renders "good" as "no ordinary child" in this verse. All parents consider their children special, but perhaps Moses' mother noted something unusual about him. Perhaps "good" is meant to suggest that Moses was a healthy boy who would likely survive, so long as the Egyptians didn't discover him.

Just what was Moses' mother trying to accomplish by placing her son in a basket made of papyrus and coated with pitch? She seemed to have hidden him in their home for as long as she could. To avoid detection, she put him in the basket and placed it among the reeds along the riverbank. There among the flowing water and rustling reeds, the baby's cries would be harder to detect. Although the reeds would keep the basket from floating downstream, they would also make the child more vulnerable to crocodile attack, but some risks had to be taken. In effect, Moses' mother trusted her son to God's providence. She had done all she could to preserve this boy's life; his survival was ultimately up to God.

That a kindhearted daughter of Pharaoh happened to choose this location to bathe and that she happened to locate the basket (Ex. 2:5) suggests God had taken up the responsibility for protecting Moses. The princess recognized immediately this baby was an Israelite, perhaps because he was (presumably) circumcised or because there could be no other reason to place one's son in a basket in the river other than to spare his life. Maybe God even used the child's cries to soften her heart and prompt her to adopt him. Her split-second decision played into God's long-term plan to provide Moses with the very best of Egyptian culture, an investment that would pay dividends throughout his leadership of the Israelites.

The story of Moses' deliverance is told with irony and deep significance. Several terms appear here that connect this story with earlier events or which will figure prominently later. The word rendered "basket" (v. 3) is only used one other time in the Old Testament, to describe Noah's ark (Gen. 6:14). Noah's version of the ark may have been larger, but God used both to preserve these men from destruction for the sake of the greater good. The word rendered "tar" in Exodus 2:3 has already been used in 1:14, in describing the Israelites' forced labor with mortar and bricks. The basket was placed among the "reeds" of the Nile (2:3); many years later the Israelites would cross the "Sea of Reeds."

Pharaoh had intended the Nile to be a place of death (see 1:22), but it plays a significant role in Moses' deliverance. Pharaoh had allowed the Israelite daughters to live, and it was an Israelite daughter (Moses' sister) who helped arrange for Moses to be kept with his family for two to three years until he was weaned. It was none other than Pharaoh's own daughter who adopted Moses, permitting not just any Israelite male to live but the very one who would liberate all Israelites. What is more, this liberator was raised and educated at Pharaoh's expense. How ironic that the king's desperate Plan D (1:22) actually fostered Israel's deliverance. How ironic that those who had spoiled the mighty Pharaoh's most extreme plans were all women: the midwives, Moses' mother and sister, and Pharaoh's daughter. Earlier we noticed that the narrator provided the midwives' names but not Pharaoh's (1:15). We see a similar phenomenon in this story as well. All the characters go unnamed until the end of the story when we are told the name of the little boy but no one else. The names of the others, at least of Moses' mother and sister, are known and are provided later (see Num. 26:59). The one character whose name we never learn is the daughter of Pharoah, the most powerful man in the ancient Near East.

There is irony, too, in the name given to Moses. It is an Egyptian name meaning "son" or "one who is born" and forms other names like Thutmose and Ahmose. This name also sounds very much like the Hebrew word for "drawn out" (*mashah*), an apt description of the moment his life was providentially preserved for greater service. Throughout his life, Moses would carry about this dual citizenship as he employed the education and life skills he had developed at

Egypt's expense on behalf of his true people. He would one day need to choose which identity to embrace—that of his birth or of his foster family. The latter offered the best of culture and comfort; the former afforded an opportunity to participate in God's plan to redeem humanity but only if he was willing to embrace the service and suffering this required.

MOSES' FIRST ATTEMPT AT DELIVERING ISRAELITES

At some point Moses became aware that he was a native Israelite. That awareness may have sprung from early memories, hearing his parents discuss God's ancient promises to their ancestors: Abraham, Isaac, and Jacob. Perhaps the details of his rescue had become more widely known. There were probably many in the king's court who were quick to remind Moses he was not really Egyptian.

How Moses learned of his true heritage remains unclear, but at some point he chose to investigate matters more intently. Exodus 2:11 pictures him going out to see where the Israelites were forced to work. The repetition of the phrase "his own people" (literally "his brothers") implies that Moses had a keen interest in the fate of his kinsmen. Upon witnessing a graphic instance of an Israelite being mistreated, Moses struck and killed the offending Egyptian. That he first looked about to make sure there were no other witnesses indicates he intended his blow to kill. That he buried the corpse shows awareness of his guilt. Moses' motive may have been good—to deliver this beleaguered brother—but his actions betrayed a violent, power-driven mind-set.

The next day, when Moses encountered another example of violence, this time Israelite on Israelite, Moses once again intervened on behalf of the weaker party. The aggressor's reply stung and startled Moses. His authority, both as a member of the king's royal family and as a fellow Israelite, was rejected. Furthermore, Moses' misdeed had already become known, making him no more than a criminal himself. The man's challenge—"Who made you ruler and judge over us?" (v. 14)—would be repeated more than once by the Israelites against Moses in the years to come. Although the man's words were meant to wound Moses, they also warned him, allowing him time to flee Egypt (v. 15).

MOSES IN MIDIAN

Moses sought refuge in Midian. This geographic term refers to various locations, all to the east of Egypt, but west, north, and east of the Gulf of Aqaba. Canaan was closer, but the shortest route there would have taken him by fortified Egyptian outposts along the way of the sea. Canaan was also under Egyptian control while Midian was autonomous.

One day, while sitting near a well, Moses noticed several shepherd girls filling water troughs for their flocks. As soon as the troughs were full, other shepherds pushed the girls aside. At this point, Moses intervened, chased off the bullies, and then watered the girls' flocks. Here again we see Moses' desire for justice exercising itself with sufficient force to chase off the oppressors who outnumbered him. The narrator described Moses' deliverance of the girls using a verb rich with significance for his future role: he "came to their rescue" (2:17). Here he rescued—literally "saved"—a few helpless individuals, but later God would use him to save a nation (14:30).

This harassment must have been a regular occurrence that frequently delayed the girls' return home, for their father was surprised at how early they returned. When he asked what happened, they relayed the story of their Egyptian rescuer. The narrator moved quickly from an invitation to dinner to a marriage with one of the daughters to the birth of a son, Gershom. In the naming of his firstborn, Moses revealed the longing of his heart for his homeland, saying, "I have become a foreigner in a foreign land" (2:22). Whether he was conscious of it or not, this name also identified the situation of his own people, Israel. They, too, were exiles in a foreign land, a situation God would use Moses to resolve.

ISRAEL'S PLIGHT

Exodus 2 closes with a return to the plight of these Israelites. By now they had languished for a "long period" (v. 23) under oppressive Egyptian policies. The old king has died—the one who sought Moses' life—and a new king has taken the throne. But the same oppressive policies against the Israelites persisted (v. 23). The purpose of these verses is twofold: to describe Israel's response to their condition and God's reaction to them. According to Exodus 2:23, the Israelites "groaned . . . and cried out" because of their slavery. The first of these terms can be used to describe the agonizing moans of a woman in hard labor (see Jer. 22:23) or of a starving person (see Lam. 1:11). Although they had suffered for some time, this is the first time in Exodus that the Israelites called out to God for deliverance.

And God heard. In fact, the narrator piled up verbs to describe God's impassioned reaction: "God heard . . . remembered . . . looked on . . . and was concerned about" the Israelites (Ex. 2:24–25). What

God heard was "their groaning" (v. 24), which is a different word from the one appearing in verse 23. God remembered the covenant he had made with Abraham, Isaac, and Jacob, in which he had committed himself to looking after their descendants. God had told Abraham he would deliver the Israelites from their captivity and punish their captives (see Gen. 15:14). To say that God looked on the Israelites is not to suggest he had ever lost sight of them. All these terms are anthropomorphisms, which picture God using human terms. God had been aware of their plight all along. A more literal translation of Exodus 2:25 would read, "God saw the Israelites, and God knew." The New International Version renders the last phrase as an expression of God's concern ("was concerned about them") while the New Living Translation supplies an object (God "knew it was time to act"). Other translations render the phrase as "took notice" (NRSV, NASB). The English Standard Version stays closest to the original with "God saw the people of Israel—and God knew." The abruptness of this phrase in the original language strengthens the connection with the events of Exodus 3 and makes clear that when God acts, it is from perfect knowledge.

PREPARATION OF A FAITHFUL SERVANT

How do the events of these two chapters provide insight into this man, who would become a faithful servant in God's house? Moses' deliverance from certain death through the hand of Providence must have marked him from his earliest days. His family likely retold this miracle many times during Moses' time at home. Such an experience often produces a sense of special destiny, of having been set apart for a purpose. John Wesley's young life was spared from a fire in his home. Years afterward he would speak of himself as a "brand plucked from the burning." This moment seemed to fuel the passion with which he preached across England, Ireland, and Scotland. Wesley was holding a watch night service on February 9, 1750, and realized that it was forty years to the day and hour when he was taken out of the flames. He wrote in his journal that upon realizing this, he "stopped, and gave a short account of that wonderful providence. The voice of praise and thanksgiving went up on high, and great was our rejoicing before the Lord." One of his biographers explains that "both he and the Methodist people knew by that time for what blessed work he had been spared."[2]

I know a young man from Haiti whose life was miraculously spared four times before his first birthday. He was abandoned as nonviable at birth until a nurse heard him crying and rushed him to the nursery. A week later the car in which he was riding was involved in an accident, and his body was hurled out the window. A street vendor picked him up and carried him to a hospital, where he was treated. Some months after this, he was scalded when a pot of boiling water tipped onto his back. Later, he contracted typhoid fever and was in a coma. His father prayed that God would spare this boy's life, and God answered that prayer. The boy's parents, recognizing the clear evidence of God's providence, rededicated their son to God's purposes. Today he is an ordained minister, holds a PhD in New Testament studies, and teaches young men and women the truths of God's Word. This is how he describes the effect of providential deliverance on his life: "I grew up with an acute awareness that God's hand was on my life and the fact that I should have died but God said 'live.' So, I consider each day to be an opportunity to give back to God the life that he has given me."

A second consequence of Moses' early deliverance would have been a deep trust in God's providence. One of John Wesley's biographers explained the effect of Wesley's rescue this way: "There was no place found in his thought from that time onward for a doubt of a Supreme Being whose mercy interposes in moments of danger."[3] Moses' experience likely produced the same confidence. How helpful this confidence would have been when faced with Pharaoh's repeated refusals, the looming obstacle of the Red Sea, a wilderness with little water and food, and less-than-reliable followers.

A third consequence of Moses' deliverance may be less obvious than the first two: the connection of his life with figures from Israel's past. Moses' early life bears a striking resemblance to those of Joseph and Hagar. Both Joseph and Moses were spared death by being lifted out of something dangerous, a pit for Joseph and the Nile for Moses. A close relative of both men was instrumental in their deliverance (Joseph's brother, Reuben, and Moses' sister, Miriam), and non-Israelites played a role in the deliverance of both. Each married the daughter of a priest and fathered two sons. Moses' life is also similar to that Hagar. The life of each is marked by a dramatic shift in roles. Hagar went from being an Egyptian slave to Abraham's wife; Moses began as the child of Hebrew slaves but became the son of an Egyptian princess. Both Hagar and Moses fled hostility and, in the midst of their flights, encountered God (Hagar in Gen. 16:7 and Moses at the burning bush in Ex. 3:2). During this encounter, both were instructed to return, and both received a promise (Gen. 16:11–12; Ex. 3:12).[4]

The association with these earlier figures is more than a novelty. We have every reason to believe their stories would have been told to Moses by his parents. Seeing the connection between his life and earlier heroes would have renewed his confidence in God's promises to Israel and in God's character as he who delivers the outcast.

A fourth consequence of Moses' deliverance involved his Egyptian upbringing. Because a daughter of the pharaoh raised him,

Moses would have received the best of Egyptian learning and culture, which was considerable. Egypt was one of the most advanced cultures of its time, and Moses was given access to the best it had to offer. In addition to the knowledge and skills he would have acquired, he would have grown in self-confidence. Little did he know at the time that God would use all this to help him lead God's people. Later we will see how the Israelites plundered Egypt as they left, but Moses' upbringing shows that the plundering actually began much earlier.

These early experiences reveal an important aspect of Moses' character: a strong sense of justice. One commentator, Terence E. Fretheim, has noted that Moses challenged three types of injustice in Exodus 2: first, the beating of an Israelite slave by an Egyptian master (v. 11); second, the wronging of one Hebrew toward another (v. 13); and third, the oppression of women by male shepherds (v. 17). Fretheim points out that Moses took into his own hands the need to enforce justice. Moses received his sense of justice not from his Israelite heritage but from his Egyptian training.[5] But Moses' efforts at producing justice were largely failures. While two men were spared beatings, another was murdered and Moses himself was forced to flee for his life. Perhaps this experience alerted Moses to how even the best intentions can backfire. Such a lesson would help prepare him to do God's work in God's way.

Not all of the benefits gained during these early years would have been immediately understood as blessings. To be separated from his family of origin must have been terribly difficult for Moses, as well as for his family. That experience stamped Moses with a deep sense of alienation. We see that in the naming of his firstborn, Gershom, whose name was chosen because Moses was "a foreigner in a foreign land" (v. 22). This feeling was caused by something deeper than merely being an Egyptian living in Midian; Moses was likely unable to fully identify with any culture. He was born an Israelite, raised as an Egyptian, but forced to live in Midian.

Yet God used even this sense of rootlessness in Moses' life. While his fellow Israelites would struggle to shake off centuries of slavery, Moses needed no convincing that he and his people were made for something better. Perhaps this very feeling of alienation helped him take on the mantle of leadership, setting him apart from God's people to lead them better. Exposure to multiple cultures certainly broadened Moses' perspective, enabling him to better interpret and flex with the challenges and opportunities that would come.

CONCLUSION

As these first two chapters conclude, the Israelites cried out to God who listens with deep compassion. How would he respond to their need? Unlikely as it might seem, this Moses who was born to the Israelites but raised by the Egyptians, a failed savior, a murderer and fugitive, a shepherd living far from Egypt and from his people, had been perfectly prepared by Yahweh to faithfully lead God's people out of slavery. A dramatic summons for this task was soon to come, complete with burning bush. This encounter would not only draft Moses into God's plan but also further prepare him for service.

2

Calling the Faithful Servant, Part 1

Exodus 3

Some chapter divisions in the Bible obscure as much as they reveal. Exodus 3 is one of those cases. While it is helpful to know that chapter 3 introduces a significant shift in the story of Israel's deliverance, it is important to recognize that this shift occurs because of what we read in the closing verses of chapter 2. Because "God looked on the Israelites and was concerned about them" (2:25), God led Moses to the burning bush. All that occurs in this chapter and the following chapter of this book takes place because of God's concern for Israel. God so loved his people that he sent Moses. The encounter at the bush was Moses' call to his role as God's servant. It was also an opportunity for God to teach Moses several important lessons about what it meant to be a servant of the God whose name Moses was about to learn.

ENCOUNTER AT THE BURNING BUSH

While serving his father-in-law as a shepherd, Moses discovered his true vocation: servant of Yahweh. Exodus 2 concluded with a description of God's compassion for his suffering people and his intention to intervene on their behalf. Exodus 3 begins that intervention with the selection of the man who would, humanly speaking, shepherd God's people from a place of danger to one of safety and abundance (see Isa. 63:11). While Moses was caring for helpless creatures, God called him to care for his suffering flock.

Moses had taken the sheep to graze in the wilderness near Mount Sinai (here called Horeb). God likely chose this site because it was to this mountain the Israelites would later come to worship him (see Ex. 3:12). It must have been a comfort for Moses to lead the Israelites to the place where he himself had encountered God. Even in the early days of the exodus, leading the Israelites was challenging. At least Moses knew that their initial destination was a place where he had already spoken with God.

Although we cannot be certain whether to speak of this as a journey "to the far side of the wilderness" (3:1), "to the backside of the desert" (KJV), "to the west side of the wilderness" (ESV), "beyond the wilderness" (NRSV), "far into the wilderness" (NLT), "deep into the steppe,"[1] or "after grassland,"[2] the journey was likely some distance from Moses' home. Such long journeys were necessary to obtain pastureland for the sheep.

That Yahweh appeared to Moses so far from home was part of God's lesson for his servant. God knew where Moses was and could meet him there, even this far from Jethro's house. God is able to reach anyone, anywhere, at any time, even in the "far side of the wildnerness." God can always find us, but will he find us available to him?

While tending sheep in the wilderness, Moses saw a burning thorn bush. The Hebrew term used to describe this type of bush is only used two other times in the Old Testament. One likely alludes back to this passage (Deut. 33:16) while the other describes a rocky crag (1 Sam. 14:4). This word is closely related to another Hebrew word meaning "tooth." One commentator identifies this bush as *rubus sanctus* or holy thorn bush,[3] while another considers it *rubus discolor* or blackberry.[4]

Moses may have witnessed such a phenomenon before because lightning strikes could easily have kindled dry shrubs. What caught his attention was that though the bush was burning it was not consumed. The bush remained whole even in the midst of the flames. Moses did not yet know that he was witnessing a theophany, a visible manifestation of the presence of God, but we do because the narrator informed us that "the angel of the LORD" was in the bush (Ex. 3:2).

Of all the ways God might have chosen to call Moses into his service, why through a bush that burned? God used this device to teach Moses several things about being a faithful servant in God's house. Since a burning bush was not an unknown phenomenon, a casual observer might easily overlook it. The one who turned aside to look more closely would find his life forever changed (v. 3 KJV). Jesus emphasized the same principle in his parables: "Whoever has ears to hear, let them hear" (Mark 4:9).

The bush that burned but was not consumed also illustrated the destiny of God's chosen people. They had endured years of servitude in the furnace of Egypt but were not consumed (see Deut. 4:20; 1 Kings 8:51; Jer. 11:4). As God was in the midst of this bush, preserving it from destruction, so he was with his people in their adversity. God's plan for them was still in effect, a plan in which Moses—himself preserved through the fires of affliction—was about to assume the key role as God's servant. This realization had a profound impact on Moses.

Moses was also meant to realize it was God's presence that kept the bush from being consumed by fire. No matter the challenge, God's presence is all one requires. Apparently, Moses learned this lesson. Toward the end of his life, while pronouncing a final blessing on God's people, this servant referred to God as "him who dwelt in the burning bush" (Deut. 33:16).

As Moses approached the burning bush, God called to him from within it but forbade Moses to come closer and commanded him to remove his shoes (Ex. 3:4–5). In this way, too, God taught Moses an important lesson: although too holy for casual access, God makes himself available to the humble. God would not allow his holiness to be taken for granted, but he graciously allowed his servant to come near. God also demonstrated his ability to sanctify any place. In the ancient Near East, the wilderness was seen as an unholy place, but even that became holy ground when God was present. An ordinary bush became extraordinary by God's presence, and an unholy place was sanctified.

Once Moses demonstrated his submission to God by removing his sandals, God revealed his identity. He is the God of Moses' father, Amram, but also the God of Abraham, Isaac, and Jacob (v. 6). With this self-description, God linked the past and present. He connected Moses, the fugitive shepherd, both with his family in Egypt and with the Israelites' ancestors. If Moses was to be a faithful servant in God's household, he would need to understand its roots traced back to Abraham—and he was part of it. Although Moses felt like an alien in a strange land, God recognized him as an Israelite, one of the chosen people.

That these lessons are learned barefoot is also significant. To be without sandals was to be vulnerable, unable to run away, humbled before a greater power. Joshua would later learn the same lesson (see Josh. 5:15). Just as God was able to sanctify this bush and the ground around it, setting it apart for his purpose, so God could set apart Moses for holy use, but only if he remained humble. Later we learn that Moses was a man of great humility (see Num. 12:3); perhaps this experience helped to make him so.

Moses' reacted to this revelation was fear, averting his gaze (Ex. 3:6). Perhaps this was an expression of reverence because he realized God is too holy to look at. When his relationship with God grew, Moses sought the opportunity to see God (see Ex. 33:18). Moses' fear may also have arisen from the thought of what this encounter might mean for his future.

GOD ENLISTED MOSES

Moses had good cause to fear, for God was about to summon him to the task of rescuing the Israelites from Egypt. Moses responded to this summons with a series of questions and objections. God answered each one, for the most part patiently, and Moses finally accepted the mission. The initial call comes in Exodus 3:7–10, where God stated emphatically that he had seen Israel's misery (v. 7). Their cries in the midst of oppression had reached his ears in heaven and prompted his concern for their "suffering" (v. 7). This word can mean either suffering in general or physical pain in particular. The latter sense is used in Ezekiel 28:24 to describe the pain one feels from contact with a thorn bush. Perhaps this is another reason God chose a thorn bush for this theophany.

In the initial summons, God taught his servant yet another lesson. To be faithful in God's house, Moses would need to know how much God cared about his household (see Ex. 3:16–17; 4:31). The Lord needed a shepherd after his own heart (see Jer. 3:15), one who would lead Israel with the same compassion God himself felt for them. Moses possessed this quality, remaining remarkably patient with the Israelites, always willing to intercede for them.

When Moses heard the opening phrase of Exodus 3:8, he may have breathed a sigh of relief because it seemed to indicate that God would do the work of freeing the people. God said, "I have come down to rescue them . . . and to bring them up . . . into a good and spacious land," because he had heard their cry and seen their misery (vv. 8–9). Note the artistry of this passage, how verse 9 essentially repeats the message of verse 7 but reverses the verb order. Hebrew narrators often employed this technique, known as *chiasm*. Whatever relief Moses may have felt at being off the hook was quickly snatched away when God said in verse 10, "Now go."

God had seen the suffering of his people and had descended to deliver them, but this deliverance would come through Moses. This is one of the central requirements for God's servant: to devote oneself to God's work, serving as his spokesman and instrument. God's servant is not self-employed but is engaged in the Master's business. Deliverance would come about as Moses confronted Pharaoh himself (v. 10). There would be no secret escape under the cover of darkness; it would come only after a head-to-head confrontation with the mighty Egyptian king. While the verb in verse 10 is translated as an infinitive: "to bring my people . . . out of Egypt," it is probably best rendered as an imperative: "You must lead my people Israel out of Egypt" (NLT).

No wonder Moses balked. "Who am I," he asked, "that I should go to Pharaoh?" (v. 11). Moses' first question rose from his sense of inadequacy. He knew himself, a middle-aged shepherd with a criminal record. How did that prepare him to confront Pharaoh and liberate slaves? Actually it didn't; on the contrary, it disqualified more than qualified him. This may be why God said nothing about Moses' qualifications for the job in response to the question. Instead, God assured Moses, saying, "I will be with you" (v. 12). Apparently it mattered little who Moses was, only whether God was with him. God does not read résumés.

God also offered a sign that he was the one sending Moses (v. 12). God's words may mean the proof that he called Moses would be the fact he returned to this site with the Israelites to worship, but this does not seem to prove much. Furthermore, it would do little to encourage Moses when encouragement would be most needed. Confronting Pharaoh, convincing the reluctant Israelites, enduring delay, facing the Egyptian army while trapped with their backs against the Red Sea, wandering without water in the wilderness—these are times when a sign would have been most welcome.

What God did was give Moses a divine guarantee of success. The "sign" is not what *would* happen—that they would eventually reach Mount Sinai—but what *just* happened—God gave his promise that this would occur. The sign was not a letter Moses had to wait to open until he returned to that spot; it was a spoken promise from the Lord that he could recall whenever his faith lagged. Just as we look to the sign of the rainbow in the sky (which is described using the same Hebrew word used here) as assurance God will not destroy the earth with a flood (see Gen. 9:12), Moses could reflect on God's promise of eventual success to gain encouragement in the difficult days that laid ahead. This mission could only fail if God ceased to be God.

Moses responded to this promise by asking what he should tell the Israelites if they wanted to know the name of the One who sent him (Ex. 3:13). Behind Moses' question was a deeper one: Who is this God who just gave this great promise? After all, the value of a promise depends on the character of the one promising. Moses wanted an answer for Israel's sake and for his own as well.

In the ancient world, knowing a god's name made it possible to communicate with that god, perhaps to make an appeal. Some used the names of deities for manipulation, thinking that the god could be controlled through incantations or curses. We have no reason to suspect that Moses' motives were manipulative. He simply wanted to know who was making this promise in order to give greater confidence to himself and anyone else who wanted to know.

Moses may have had an additional motive for asking. As a child he likely heard the story of his ancestor, Jacob. After an all-night wrestling match with a "man," Jacob discovered he had actually "struggled with God" (Gen. 32:28). Jacob refused to let go of the opponent until he learned his name. But God refused to identify himself, blessed Jacob, and left. Perhaps Moses was hoping for the same treatment—not having his hip wrenched out of joint (see 32:25)—but God's blessing and blessed departure, leaving Moses once again to mind his own business.

Moses was not alone among biblical characters in his reluctance to accept God's call. When Gideon (Judg. 6:15), Isaiah (Isa. 6:5), and Jeremiah (Jer. 1:6) received God's call, they too bemoaned their inadequacies. Amos made it clear to his detractors that being a prophet was not his idea but God's (Amos 7:14–15). One suspects that many of God's servants have said something similar, given the challenges of being in God's employ.

If Moses did hope to be excused with a blessing and blessed departure, he was disappointed. God answered Moses' request for a name by identifying himself more fully than ever before. Not even Abraham received this much information about the identity of God. This is not the only time God accommodated himself to a challenge. Abraham's questioning response to God's promise of descendants produced an even greater revelation of God's plan (see Gen. 15). The same was true for Job, who was given a whirlwind tour of God's activity only *after* he summoned God to court (see Job 13). God does not tolerate faithless impertinence, but he honors the faithful questioner.

Exodus 3 contains God's fullest self-revelation up to this point in Scripture, yet it is still difficult to comprehend. God identified himself using a form of the Hebrew verb "to be" (*yhwh* or *Yahweh*). This is often translated "I AM" (v. 14) but could instead be rendered "I will be." God first identified himself with a phrase based on this verb: "I AM WHO I AM" (ESV, NASB, NLT, NRSV) or "I am he who is" (NJB). Then he used just the verb, saying that Moses should reply to any questioners: "I AM has sent me to you" (v. 14). In other words, God named himself by describing himself. One commentator explains that in place of a label, God provided a theology.[5]

At the heart of this theology is God's ever-present faithfulness and his nature as eternal yet personal. God always is, was, and will be himself. He has never not been, and he will never not be. He will never act out of character or lack the qualities that make him who he is. He can always be depended upon and will never disappoint. Moses sought a name, but God gave him much more: a guarantee. What an important lesson this was for the one called to become a faithful servant in God's house. Knowing God as ever-present faithfulness enabled Moses to remain full of faith, to stretch his staff over the Red Sea, to strike the rock and produce water, to promise more bread and meat than the Israelites would be able to eat, to continue to trust through decades of wandering, and to insist on a bright future if Israel remained faithful.

Even as God revealed himself to Moses, he indicated how much more there was to know. To know God is to know how little one knows of God. The greatest lesson we can learn about him is that we have much more to learn. Theologians refer to this as God's inscrutability; he is knowable, yet not fully knowable. Thomas Aquinas, who had one of the great theological and philosophical minds of all time, wrote a detailed description of all we can know of God's existence and nature. In the end, however, he had to conclude "the more perfectly do we know God in this life, the more we understand that he surpasses all that the mind comprehends."[6]

Having granted Moses' request to know God's name, God then repeated his command and provided further direction, even giving Moses the words to say to the Israelites. God began by linking a shorthand version of the name he just provided with the more descriptive title he used before: "Yahweh, the God of your fathers, the God of Abraham, the God of Isaac, and the God of Jacob" (v. 15, author translation). In verse 15, God used the third person form of the verb "to be" rather than the first person form used in verse 14: "he will be" rather than "I will be."[7] By connecting the name Yahweh with the God worshiped by their ancestors, God gave the Israelites great reason for hope. They have not been forgotten. The same God who brought them miraculously into being through Abraham, Isaac, and Jacob is the ever-faithful One now ready to intervene in their struggles. What is more, Yahweh had great plans for them, hence his reference to being with them "forever" and "from generation to generation" (v. 15).

God provided even more direction to Moses (vv. 16–17). He was to gather the Israelite elders and inform them that this God, Yahweh, was very concerned about what had been done to them in Egypt (literally "concerned I am concerned"). He intended to liberate them from their bondage and give them their own homeland, the land of Canaan. The good news was that this is the very land promised to their ancestor Abraham. It was a land "flowing with milk and honey" (v. 17), meaning there was plenty of pasturage for sheep and goats and plenty of date palms from which to derive

CALLING THE FAITHFUL SERVANT, PART 1

syrup. Bee honey was known in ancient Israel but was far less common than date syrup. The bad news was that this land was occupied by several nations that would not likely leave without a fight.

In addition to revealing his name and giving Moses a script, God predicted what would happen when Moses met with the Israelite elders (vv. 18–22). They would listen to Moses (v. 18), go together to Pharaoh (v. 18), and announce to him that Yahweh, the God of the Hebrews (the term used for the Israelites in international contexts), had appeared to them. They would request permission to go away briefly to offer sacrifices to Yahweh (v. 18), and Pharaoh would flatly refuse (v. 19). God emphasized he already knew of the king's refusal and no amount of human might would persuade him to change his mind. The final phrase in verse 19, literally "not with a mighty hand," probably does not refer to divine power as suggested by many translations, including the New International Version's "unless a mighty hand compels him." The meaning is better captured in the King James Version: "And I am sure that the king of Egypt will not let you go, no, not by a mighty hand." If this is the right way to understand it, this may have been a mild rebuke of Moses' tendency to revert to violence to bring about justice.

The only might that would move Pharaoh was God's might, and that would be demonstrated as he stretched out his hand to strike Egypt with mighty wonders (v. 20). God promised that after a divinely inflicted beating, Pharaoh would not merely allow the Israelites to go but would send them away, happy to be rid of them. As a bonus, the effect of the divine pummeling would so impress the Egyptians (a very religious people, quick to recognize divine power) that they would even pay the Israelites to leave (v. 21). The Israelite women were to ask for silver, gold, and clothing from their Egyptian neighbors. That the instruction was given to the women was likely a further insult to the Egyptians, who so prized masculine power that they portrayed their enemies as women. Even Israelite women would be able to plunder the Egyptians. The Israelites would then clothe their sons and daughters with the plunder. Ancient cultures, unlike our own, did not consider children the most important members of society. Dressing the children in jewelry and nicer clothing would emphasize the abundance of the Israelites' possessions (v. 22).

God's call sometimes comes with a general sense of what awaits his servant. Rarely does his call come with this clear a prediction of what is to follow. God told Moses what laid ahead for several reasons. First, it made clear that God can foretell the future and therefore can be trusted. Consider how this would help Moses, God's servant, to trust his divine but unpredictable Master. Second, this specific predication of events made it clear that Pharaoh would eventually give in and give the order to depart. Although Moses and the Israelites still became discouraged, their discouragement would have been more pronounced and more debilitating had they not known what God already knew. Third, this predication made it clear to God's servant that the deliverance of the Israelites was God's work, to be done in God's way.

CONCLUSION

God so loved Israel that he called Moses. Summoned into God's service, Moses responded with a series of questions that continue into Exodus 4. God also began to teach Moses important lessons about what it means to be his servant. Most of the lessons in this chapter revolve around a central truth: God is ever-present. This God might appear anywhere, even on the backside of the desert, and in any form, even a burning bush. The one who took the trouble to step aside and see what God was doing would discern God's presence where he might seem to be absent. The presence of God changes everything. It can preserve a bush from incineration and a people from destruction. It can transform a middle-aged murderer into a powerful leader. This leader would need to understand, however, that the ever-present God is holy and makes holy whatever and whomever he chooses. This God welcomes questions from a willing heart but will tolerate nothing less than obedience to his plan. In return, he issues a promise of success.

This God is always present not as a spy but as one who is concerned for his people. Those who serve him best are those who love his people as he does. His is a faithful presence, unlimited by time.

Exodus 3 portrays God as active in the present, having been active in the past, and intending to be active in the future. A faithful servant must recognize the eternal nature of the Master and realize that there is always more to learn about the Master.

Calling the Faithful Servant, Part 2

EXODUS 4

God's purpose in appearing to Moses in the burning bush was not merely to call him to the task of leading Israel out of slavery. It was also to teach Moses important lessons about what it means to be a faithful servant of God. He wanted Moses to understand that God's presence is all that is necessary and that it can always be relied upon. It was this presence that had kept Israel from being consumed in the furnace of Egypt and would liberate them to carry out their mission of blessing the nations. In part two of Moses' encounter with God at the burning bush, the lessons continue as do Moses' questions and concerns.

MOSES' THIRD QUESTION AND GOD'S ANSWER

Moses' third question concerns the success of his mission. He was not sure the Israelites would listen to him or believe he actually received this summons from God. Some translations, such as the

English Standard Version, present this as an assertion rather than a question: "But behold, they will not believe me or listen to my voice, for they will say, 'The LORD did not appear to you'" (Ex. 4:1).

What prompted his pessimism? Was Moses thinking about his own misguided attempts at bringing justice and how they failed to win Israel's support (see 2:11–15)? Was he aware of others who had tried and failed to rally the Israelites to freedom? Was he reflecting the despair of his people, too beaten down by Egyptian oppression and divine silence to dare to hope? Or was this simply one more excuse to avoid going?

Whatever Moses' motives, God replied by giving him a series of signs he could perform to persuade the Israelites that he did indeed speak for God. If Moses' question/assertion reflected his own failure, it is significant that God's response involved things Moses must do which could not be accomplished without God's help. Moses may have failed before, but that was partly because he acted on his own. With God's presence and pursued in the right way, another outcome to the venture was likely. And if Moses' question/assertion reflected his doubt that the Israelites could be convinced, it is interesting that what God proposes to do are not major miracles. We later see the Egyptian magicians replicate two of them (see 7:11–12, 22). God seemed to think the Israelites were closer to believing Moses' message than Moses himself imagined.

The first of these signs was to turn Moses' staff into a snake, then back to a staff (4:2–4). Once while in Mozambique, I noticed a bird fluttering at something in a bush. The gardener also noticed and moved cautiously toward the bush, machete in hand. He began slashing at the bush, careful to keep from getting too close. I wondered at his caution until I learned he was slashing at a green mamba, an extremely poisonous snake. The gardener's reaction to that snake reminds me of how Moses responded to what he must have recognized from his

CALLING THE FAITHFUL SERVANT, PART 2

years in the wilderness as a poisonous snake: He jumped away. At God's direction, however, Moses grabbed it by the tail. This is a dangerous way to pick up a snake because it leaves the head free to strike. Moses exercised both great courage and great faith in his obedience, believing that so long as he obeyed God he had no need to worry.

God may have chosen this sign for several reasons. Snakes were powerful symbols in the ancient world. They represented fertility and immortality, perhaps because of their ability to shed their skin. They were believed to possess wisdom and were connected with healing. The symbol of the medical profession today, the caduceus, is traced to Asclepius, the Greek god of healing, whose staff was wound with snakes. Snakes could variously be seen as harmful, benign, or even helpful. The Egyptians believed that when Ra, the god of the sun, set beneath the horizon, it passed into the realm of Apophis, a serpent. This was a dangerous time, for Apophis desired to extinguish the sun forever. Another serpent, Mehen, was coiled around the boat in which the sun traveled through the darkness. His job was to protect the sun until it rose in the morning. The importance of the snake in Egypt is underscored by its inclusion in the pharaoh's crown. By demonstrating power over snakes, Moses and the God he represented communicated to the Egyptians that however powerful the snake might be, however important to Egypt's survival, God controlled it.

This miracle would also demonstrate to the Israelites, to Pharaoh, and perhaps to Moses himself, that appearances can be deceiving. What began as a harmless shepherd's staff could become a deadly snake. The Israelites might appear to be nothing more than slaves and Moses only a shepherd, but appearances can be deceiving. The Israelites are God's chosen people and Moses their divinely appointed ruler. Perhaps this is why God mentioned Abraham, Isaac, and Jacob

(v. 5), for Israel's identity as God's covenant people indicated their true potency. Moses would perform this sign before Pharaoh (see 7:9–12), the first of many proofs of Israel's true identity.

God provided a second sign in case the Israelites ignored or disbelieved the first (4:6–8). When Moses placed his hand into his robe and pulled it out, it was covered with a skin disease. Some translations identify this as leprosy, but it was probably something more like psoriasis. Whatever the precise diagnosis, later Israelite law stated that anyone who had this disease was ceremonially unclean, unable to enjoy full access to God's presence. So while Moses stood in God's presence, God rendered his servant ineligible to be there, then just as quickly healed him of his disqualifying disease. God did not just provide a confirming miracle, but he also used that miracle to teach Moses and the Israelites an important lesson: God alone determines who does and who does not have access to him. Moses may have seen himself as a has-been, a would-be redeemer now in retirement. God saw him as his servant and would speak with him face-to-face (see Deut. 34:10). The Israelites may have thought of themselves as only Egyptian slaves, but God chose them for his "treasured possession . . . a kingdom of priests and a holy nation" (Ex. 19:5–6).

God provided a third miracle in the event that the Israelites remained unconvinced after the first two. This time God told Moses what would happen but did not give him any active role to play in the miracle. This sign also became the first of the ten plagues (see 7:15–25). God taught his servant important lessons, most obviously that he, God, had the power to do many miracles. And, though God could perform these miracles without help, he chose to perform them through an obedient servant. Moses was beginning to discover that the deliverance of God's people would involve a divine-human partnership. Outside creation and providence, God almost always involves humans in his plans. This third miracle taught Moses, the Israelites, and Pharaoh that God held Egypt's destiny in his hand. The Nile River was and is the main artery of Egypt, the ribbon of life in the desert of death. If God could turn these life-giving waters into blood, Egypt was doomed. Ominously, there is no mention of reversing this sign as there had been with the first two.

MOSES' OBJECTION AND GOD'S REPLY

At that point, Moses did not ask a question but explained why he was not the right person for this job. Clearly, this task required the ability to speak in public, something Moses had never done well. We do not know the nature of Moses' speech problem, only that he was (more literally translated) "heavy of mouth and heavy of tongue" (see 4:10). Some scholars have suggested that Moses stuttered or had some other speech impediment, based in part of God's mention of physical impairments in verse 11. Others have taken Moses' words to mean that he lacked the eloquence expected in one speaking before Pharaoh or seeking to persuade the Israelites. This view finds support in God's promise that he would teach Moses what to say.

God responded with several questions of his own, all rhetorical and all expressing the same point: If God is the one who makes it possible for people to see or not see, to speak or not speak, then why would Moses be concerned about his own inadequacy? God then repeated the command to go along with his promise to accompany Moses. God promised to "be with [Moses'] mouth" (v. 12 ESV), which puts extra emphasis on the pronoun *I* in "I will help you speak and will teach you what to say." If I help you, God explained, you have all the help you need.

This question-and-answer session shaped Moses' understanding of what it meant to be God's servant. As with Abraham, God allowed Moses an opportunity engage him in dialogue, stooping to hear and respond to his objections (see Gen. 18–19). This gesture revealed God's mercy and cultivated the divine-human partnership that characterized Moses' relationship with God for more than forty years. Moses also would have realized that merely calling himself God's servant was insufficient. He had to demonstrate his submission even at a point where he felt highly inadequate (Ex. 4:10). For the second time, God reaffirmed the most important aspect of this partnership: Its potency lay in the fact that God was with Moses, a point made still one more time before the dialogue ended (v. 15).

MOSES' PLEA AND GOD'S ANSWER

Clearly, Moses did not want to accept this commission. While we might wish Moses had responded more courageously, we must admit that the task before him was daunting. Moses was supposed to persuade one of the most powerful men in the world to give up an important part of his economic engine in the name of a largely unknown God who lacked a temple or any visible image. Even if he was successful in persuading Pharaoh, Moses would still have to persuade the Israelites to leave the only land they had ever known and resettle in a land already occupied by strong nations. Then there was the problem of how to get them from Egypt to Canaan.

Moses was desperate. Having failed to talk his way out of this assignment, he baldly begged to be excused. The New Living Translation conveys Moses' desperation well: "Lord, please! Send anyone else" (v. 13). God responded angrily, the first time in the Bible we find God expressing anger at a person. Our anger is often provoked by frustration, but that can't be the cause in God's case. The plans of an all-knowing, all-powerful God cannot be foiled by human disobedience. We sometimes become angry when our authority is challenged, as when a child misbehaves in public. The real source of our anger in such cases is our pride. God never becomes angry for this reason either, since he is never proud, at least not in the negative sense of this word.

Why then did God become angry with Moses? Likely it was because Moses insisted on living beneath God's intentions. God's promised presence meant Moses had nothing to fear, would lack nothing, and would experience ultimate success in his calling. Moses refused to believe God because his fear and feelings of inadequacy blurred his vision. Moses' refusal did not harm God; it harmed Moses. God does not take harm to his children lightly, even when the harm is self-inflicted. Yes, Moses' actions insulted God, but we misunderstand God's anger if we take it as wounded pride. The one wounded in this instance is Moses.

This explains why, instead of punishing Moses, God allayed Moses' fears by providing Aaron to accompany him (v. 14). Some scholars see it as a punishment that Moses had to share the glory with his brother, but that doesn't seem much like a punishment. Moses probably found great relief in having a trusted human partner in this great venture. Others have pointed to Aaron's role in the golden calf debacle (see Ex. 33) and conjecture that if Moses had trusted God here, that sorry episode would probably have been avoided. That explanation conflates Aaron's role as spokesperson with his role as priest. Even if we blame Moses for the former, God is responsible for appointing Aaron to the priesthood (see 28:1), and it was as spiritual leader, not spokesman, that Aaron misled the Israelites regarding the golden calf.

Aaron was a blessing to Moses, not a curse. He could "speak well" (4:14) and may already been in some type of leadership among the Israelites. This is one way to understand the reference to him as a Levite.[1] Another is to see that God employed a play on the word *Levite*, which means "joined to," assuaging Moses' concerns by joining him with Aaron.[2] It seems obvious that Aaron would be "glad to see" his brother (v. 14), so why did the narrator mention it? Perhaps it was a way of expressing that Aaron would be more than happy to partner with Moses in this venture.

There would be a partnership between Moses and Aaron but not an equal one. God would direct both Moses and Aaron, telling them what to say and do. In regard to addressing the people, however, Aaron would be to Moses as a prophet is to God, that is, a spokesperson. God instructed Moses to take his shepherd's rod with him, since God would use this to perform the signs. How telling that even before God met with Moses at the burning bush, he already knew Aaron was on his way to find his brother. In fact, God had sent Aaron (see v. 27). If only Moses had believed God instead of his fears, if only he had been willing to trust God to help him speak, he would have made the happy discovery that the answer to his prayers was on its way even before the prayer had been offered.

That was only one of the lessons God taught his servant. God also reinforced the idea that one's fears are important and can be expressed to God but must not stand in the way of obedience. Those who obey God and not their fears find God generous in supplying resources, including the necessary tools and support for the job, and a picture of the future. Such provision may be on the way even before it is requested.

CALLING THE FAITHFUL SERVANT, PART 2

MOSES RETURNED TO EGYPT

This section is divided into five brief scenes. First, Moses gained permission from his father-in-law to return to Egypt (v. 18). Then he began his journey (vv. 19–23). The third scene, one of the most puzzling in the Bible, takes place at a caravansary where Moses had stopped for the night (vv. 24–26). In the fourth scene, God sent Aaron and the brothers reunite (vv. 27–28). And finally the initial meeting takes place between Moses, Aaron, and the Israelite elders (vv. 29–31).

Apparently, social conventions required Moses to gain permission from his father-in-law before leaving Midian, permission Jethro quickly granted. Moses may have concealed the purpose of his return to Egypt, implying that he would take only a brief visit to check on his family, "to see if any of them are still alive" (v. 18). Perhaps he was afraid Jethro would refuse permission if he knew the truth. The New Living Translation's rendering of this verse, "'Please let me return to my relatives in Egypt,' Moses said. 'I don't even know if they are still alive,'" suggests Moses asked permission to leave Midian for good. That would explain why Moses took his wife and sons with him (v. 20).

The narrator focused on God's instructions to Moses (vv. 19–23) more than on the travels. God assured Moses that at least one reason for fear has been eliminated with the death of those who sought his life (v. 19). Moses had received this news while in Midian, but we do not know when. It could have been prior to his experience at the burning bush, but it seems more likely to have come either during that conversation or, more likely still, after Moses had accepted the mission. God often waits to remove obstacles until we begin to obey. The picture of Moses in verse 20 is of a caring husband and father, placing Zipporah and their two sons on a donkey so they did not have to walk, and of an obedient servant, taking along his staff as God had commanded, even though he had no sheep yet.

The instructions in verses 21–23 may have been given at some other time, perhaps along with those provided in 3:18–20. The narrator may have included them here to signal God's ongoing guidance of his servant. Moses should not have been discouraged at Pharaoh's refusal but should have recognized that the king's hardness of heart was God's doing, not an indication of failure. Moses needed to remain courageous in the face of Pharaoh's refusal and remain faithful to carry out the miraculous signs God directed. God alluded to the tenth plague by referring to Israel as his firstborn son (4:22) and threatening Pharaoh to either release Israel or risk losing his own firstborn son (v. 23). These instructions helped Moses understand an important lesson about being God's servant: The right goal sought at the wrong time or by the wrong means is the wrong goal. Moses had tried to deliver his people, but the timing was wrong and so were his methods. The timing was now right, for God had sent him. The methods would be right too, for they were of God's design.

The third episode is perplexing because it speaks of God trying to kill the very person he had just recruited. This passage is easier to understand when we remember that if God really wanted to kill Moses, then Moses would have died. Clearly this incident is reported in anthropomorphic language and does not indicate God's intention to kill Moses.

The question remains why God would even appear to be trying to kill Moses. There is also some question about whether it was Moses or Gershom, Moses' son, who was the intended target. The New International Version supplies Moses, but a more literal translation shows the ambiguity of the original: "And it came to pass on the way at the lodging-place, that Jehovah met him, and sought to kill him" (v. 24 ASV). Those who consider Moses the target point out that God has been addressing Moses in verses 21–23. They also note that Zipporah's words, "bridegroom of blood" (v. 24), are more appropriately applied to Moses than Gershom. Those who think God was aiming for Gershom point to the connection between verses 23 and 24. Verse 23 emphasizes God killing Pharaoh's firstborn son unless he released God's firstborn son; then in verse 24, God "tried" to kill "him." In both verses, scholars say, God spoke of killing a firstborn: Pharaoh's in verse 23 and Moses' in verse 24.

God's target may be unclear but the reason for his anger is not: Moses had failed to circumcise his son. This should have been done when Gershom was eight days old, as God had instructed Abraham (see Gen. 17:12). Scholars speculate that Zipporah had protested and Moses acquiesced. Or perhaps the parents thought they were exempt from the requirement because they were not living among the Israelites or for some other reason. Or they may have intended to circumcise the boy later according to the practice of the Egyptians. By the Egyptian method, the foreskin was not completely removed, only slit, and this operation was not performed until much later, when the boy was closer to manhood. Whatever their reason for not circumcising Gershom, God made it clear that leaving the boy uncircumcised was unacceptable. Thanks to Zipporah's quick thinking, the danger was averted. If Moses was indeed God's target, this was not the first time his life had been saved by a woman (that is, his mother, sister, and adoptive mother). Zipporah's comment about Moses being a "bridegroom of blood" (Ex. 4:26) may be understood as criticism of her husband. If so, far worse things have been said at near-death moments. Her words can be understood in a more positive sense. Again, taking Moses as God's intended target, she may have expressed her hope that by circumcising their son, she had regained her husband.

MOSES: FAITHFUL SERVANT OF GOD

It may not seem like it, but this whole terrifying scene is a picture of God's grace to Moses. God waited to "strike" until they were "at a lodging place" (v. 24), that is, at a place where the problem could be safely rectified. Moses had clearly not taken his Israelite heritage seriously enough. He could be an effective leader of God's people only if he lived by God's instructions. As well, Moses needed a reminder that it was God, not Pharaoh, who should be feared. Being God's servant provides no exemption from the rules or excuses for failing to obey, for Moses or us. This sobering reminder to Moses on the importance of obeying God was a gracious help to the faithful servant.

The fourth scene describes the reunion between Moses and Aaron. Aaron, having been sent by God, "met Moses at the mountain of God" (v. 27). The verb *met* is the same used to describe God meeting Moses at the lodging place (v. 24). If we assume Moses was the target there, God met Moses to correct him, while Aaron met Moses to encourage him. Although they served different purposes, both meetings were divinely directed. God always knows exactly what his servants need and is faithful to provide it.

The final scene takes place in Egypt as Moses and Aaron gathered the Israelite elders (vv. 29–31). Although at first glance the meeting appears to be positive, a closer reading reveals challenges. Moses needed to perform the signs (plural), implying they did not believe him initially, requiring the first, second, and possibly the third sign as well. Aaron performed the signs, perhaps in his role as Moses' spokesman or because he was better known to the Israelites. After hearing their message and witnessing the two or three signs, the Israelites were finally convinced of God's concern for them and "they bowed down and worshiped" (v. 31). This phrase occurs two other times in the Old Testament, both marking significant occasions when the Israelites consecrated themselves to faithfully follow their God (see 1 Chron. 29:20; 2 Chron. 29:30). The liberation of the Israelites was off to a good start.

CONCLUSION

God encountered Moses at the burning bush to summon him to the task of liberating the Israelites. This encounter also marked the beginning of Moses' formal education in what it meant to be God's servant. One of the most important lessons concerned the importance of God's presence. One might lack all else, but if God is present, that is enough. From the beginning, God's presence was Israel's greatest hope.

God's presence was also Israel's greatest threat. What happened at the "lodging place on the way" (Ex. 4:24) illustrates and anticipates the danger of God's presence among a disobedient people. Later, following the calamity of the golden calf, God threatened to abandon these people, lest he might destroy them (see 33:3). God is present. For those walking in fellowship with God, there can be no better news. For those walking in disobedience, no news could be worse. This good news/bad news aspect of God's presence is an important theme throughout the history of God's people up to today. It summons each of his servants to a life of faithfulness.

4

Divine-Human Synergy

EXODUS 5–11

Exodus 5 begins with great promise. With the sounds of Israel's worship still ringing in their ears (4:31), Moses and Aaron marched directly into Pharaoh's presence and commanded the king to release the Israelites by order of Yahweh (5:1). The result: conditions immediately became worse for the Israelites and continued to decline from there. Yet just when it appeared that Moses' mission has failed, God made it clear that he and Moses were in it together, a divine-human partnership destined to succeed against all odds.

GOD DEMONSTRATED HIS SOVEREIGN POWER

The opening five verses of Exodus 5 describe Moses' initial meeting with Pharaoh. Moses and Aaron had been instructed to go to Pharaoh, along with the Israelite elders. Since no mention is made here of the latter group, one wonders whether Moses invited them or not, or perhaps they refused to go. The demanding words with which Moses and Aaron began—"Let my people go, so that they may hold a festival to me in the wilderness" (v. 1)—was not what God had commanded. They were to say, "The LORD, the God of the Hebrews, has met with us. Let us take a three-day journey into the wilderness to offer sacrifices to the LORD our God" (3:18).

The king flatly refused their demand and with good reason. He stood as the absolute sovereign in the greatest nation in the world, a nation clearly favored by the gods, who were represented everywhere and played a role in everything. Ancient Egyptians never lacked for confidence. In contrast, the Israelites were a nation of slaves. This implied a corresponding weakness in their deity—"Who is the LORD, that I should obey him?" (5:2).

Moses and Aaron tried again, this time in a more conciliatory tone: "Please let us go" (v. 3 ESV). With this they come closer to the script they had been given. The king asked who Yahweh is; Moses and Aaron provided an answer, although their description of God was far from flattering. Apparently he demands things from people, and if they do not obey—even if they are kept from obeying—this God strikes them with disaster (v. 3). Their description sounds more like one of the gods of Egypt or elsewhere in the ancient Near East but very unlike Yahweh, whose compassion had prompted him to send Moses and Aaron on their mission. Perhaps they felt they had overstepped their bounds with the initial demand and needed to try a different strategy in order to persuade Pharaoh. Their mistake was in thinking it was their job to persuade.

Pharaoh was unimpressed with Moses and Aaron and with Yahweh. He was not interested in losing a large slave labor force (v. 5), nor did he concern himself with what the Hebrew god might do to them. How little he thought of Moses and Aaron is apparent in his command, "Get back to your work!" (v. 4). Seeking to free the

Israelites *was* Moses and Aaron's divinely appointed work, but to Pharaoh they were slaves neglecting their duties.

The king did not even acknowledge that they were the Israelites' true spokesmen. He issued new orders to the Israelites, not through Moses and Aaron but through the Egyptian "slave drivers and [Israelite] overseers" (v. 6; see also v. 14.) Pharaoh wasted no time in punishing these slaves for their presumption, ordering "that same day" (v. 6) that they would no longer be given the straw needed to bind the mud used in making bricks but would still be held to the same quota (vv. 6–9). The king wanted to punish the Israelites and keep them so busy they would not have time to think about a festival.

Moses and Aaron were not included in the meeting between the overseers and Pharaoh but were left waiting outside. Now, instead of worshiping the Lord for sending Moses and Aaron, the Israelites called on the Lord to judge these two for making their lives even more miserable: "May the LORD look on you and judge you!" (v. 21). The Israelites went from gratitude at God's intention to spare their lives to fear that the Egyptians would kill them. Moses, in turn, blamed God, accusing him of making matters worse and deceiving Moses (vv. 22–23). This was not an auspicious beginning to Moses' mission.

Moses responded to the situation by questioning God, who completely ignored Moses' question and accusation (6:1–12). God knew what Moses and the Israelites saw as unmitigated disaster was exactly what needed to happen. Only apparent disaster would provide the right backdrop for God's power. The Israelites feared Pharaoh's power, but God's "mighty hand" (repeated twice in 6:1) would force the king's hand. By the time God was finished with Pharaoh, he would be eager to have them leave.

God commanded Moses to deliver an encouraging message to the Israelites, a message composed of seven phrases each beginning with "I will" (vv. 6–8). God promised first to remove the heavy burdens from their shoulders, then liberate them from slavery. Third, God promised to vindicate them for the great injustice they had experienced. The phrase "mighty acts of judgments" (v. 6) hints at the ten plagues soon to come. Next, God promised to reaffirm his covenant with this new generation, anticipating what would follow at Mount Sinai. He did so by making two more promises: "I will take you as my own people, and I will be your God" (v. 7). God's sixth promise was to "bring [them] to the land" he had promised the patriarchs (v. 8), anticipating how he would lead them through the wilderness. Finally, he promised to give them this land as their very own, a promise with a fulfillment described in the book of Joshua.

The Israelites were unimpressed. They could not believe "because of their discouragement and harsh labor" (Ex. 6:9). *Discouragement* means "shortness of spirit." Their last flickering hope, which flared briefly at Moses and Aaron's initial appearance, had died out. What is more, they labored under Pharaoh's new demands and could spare no energy to think of freedom. Undeterred, God instructed Moses to return to Pharaoh. The Israelites were without hope, Moses was without confidence, and Pharaoh was without patience; but Moses was supposed to try again. How could this do anything but make matters worse? Moses, feeling the senselessness of this strategy, asked God that very question (v. 12).

At this crucial moment, with the fate of the enterprise hanging in the balance, the narrator (seemingly) abruptly turned to the genealogy of Moses and Aaron (vv. 13–27). He did so to remind us that these same men who appeared to be failing in their mission were God's choice for the task at hand. Jacob's first two sons are mentioned, then dropped. How often in the Old Testament do we find God bypassing the firstborn, the one thought to possess the lion's share of the family strength, in favor of the younger son. God likes to demonstrate his power by choosing those less likely to succeed. The genealogy focuses on Jacob's third son, Levi, and his descendants. No mention is made of Moses' wife and sons, but we are told about Aaron's four sons and one of his grandsons. This prepares us for the period after the exodus when these men took on the important role of God's first priests. By taking this detour, the narrator highlighted God's sovereign preparation and selection of Moses and Aaron, anticipating the central role they would play in Israel's future. The Israelites' hopelessness, Moses' insecurity, and Pharaoh's power faded from view. All we see now is God's sovereign plan unfolding, for these were the men God chose.

Inserting a genealogy at this point in the story makes it clear whom God had chosen and how he had chosen to work. This would not be *The Yahweh Show*, starring God with Moses in a supporting role. Instead, God would collaborate with humans to accomplish his will. Not a single one of God's mighty plagues would take place until Moses carried out his role as ambassador to Pharaoh.

This divine-human synergy is typical of how God works. Think of Noah building the ark, Abraham beginning the nation of Israel, or Joseph preserving God's people through famine. Although an omnipotent, omniscient God has an unlimited number of ways to accomplish his will, he often partners with humans. This is why being a faithful servant of God is so important. God doesn't just want people to stand on the sidelines and tell him how great he is. He wants people to roll up their sleeves and get to work, allowing his sovereign power to work through them. Granted, God's servants could not work at all if he does not first call and gift them. That is God's grace. And that grace makes the work both possible and a necessary response.

What if Moses had given up at this discouraging moment? It must have seemed the most obvious thing to do. Yes, he had seen and heard something strange in the desert, and yes, he had thought he was supposed to rescue his people from slavery, but was he mistaken? After all, the most powerful man in the world had dismissed him as insignificant. Moses may have thought he was only making matters worse by raising the Israelites' hopes and confronting Pharaoh. He may have thought it best to chalk up the whole thing to a misunderstanding and leave while he still had his head. To his everlasting credit, Moses did not give up. He continued to believe God would accomplish his plan to redeem Israel and do so through his faithful servant. Moses remained faithful, doing what God commanded. He boldly confronted Pharaoh once again, precipitating the great contest God had foretold (7:1).

God remained faithful as well. He reasserted his promise to deliver the Israelites (6:2–8), offering his reasons for doing so, particularly his covenant with the patriarchs and his compassion for their descendants. God did not say here that he never revealed himself to the patriarchs as Yahweh, only that he would now display what it meant to have the living, faithful God fighting alongside them.

GOD DEMONSTRATED HIS SOVEREIGN POWER THROUGH PLAGUES

God is incredibly powerful, and that was made painfully clear to the Egyptians through the ten plagues. The plagues occurred in three cycles of three each, with the tenth standing apart as the coup de grâce. Each cycle was more serious than the one preceding. At the start of each cycle, Moses and Aaron confronted Pharaoh first thing in the morning. The third plague in each cycle (numbers three,

DIVINE-HUMAN SYNERGY

six, and nine) occurred without warning. Some scholars have suggested that the plagues resulted from one another. For example, when the Nile turned to blood, the frogs left the river. The death of the frogs led to an inundation of flies, and so forth. The argument for this connection grows much weaker as the plagues continue.

What is clear is how these plagues targeted the Egyptian gods. Some plagues challenged particular gods, such as the plague of darkness which was directed against the sun god, Ra. However, that close correlation is missing with some of the other plagues (for example, hail). Nevertheless, the plagues as a whole were a clear signal that Yahweh is more powerful than any and all Egyptian gods. This point is implied in Exodus 12:12 and 15:11 and made explicit by Moses' father-in-law: "Jethro was delighted to hear about all the good things the LORD had done for Israel in rescuing them from the hand of the Egyptians. He said, 'Praise be to the LORD, who rescued you from the hand of the Egyptians and of Pharaoh, and who rescued the people from the hand of the Egyptians. Now I know that the LORD is greater than all other gods, for he did this to those who had treated Israel arrogantly'" (18:9–11).

In the first plague, the water of the Nile River turned to blood (7:14–24). Moses was to confront Pharaoh at the water's edge and strike the river with his staff. Aaron would then take his staff—which had been turned into a snake and swallowed the snakes of the magicians—and wave it over other waters, presumably the many canals dug to carry the water into fields.

God seemed to have had four purposes for turning the water into blood. First, blood symbolized the suffering of his people, the suffering that had aroused divine concern. Second, this plague temporarily paralyzed Egyptian society. The Nile was Egypt's main artery, providing water for crops, navigation, fishing, watering livestock, drinking, and bathing. It was Egypt's lifeblood. Third, turning the Nile to blood was a symbol the Egyptians were familiar with. A text dating to the late Middle Kingdom, well before Moses' day, spoke of the disaster when "the river is blood, as one drinks of it one shrinks from people and thirsts for water."[1] Whether or not such a calamity had happened before, the idea of a blood-red river already flowed in their consciousness as an unmitigated disaster.

Fourth, this plague targeted Egyptian worship because they worshiped the Nile River through the god Hapi.[2] This plague may have targeted Egyptian worship in yet another way. The phrase "in vessels [or things] of wood and stone" (v. 19) may refer to the statues of the gods. One act of Egyptian worship involved washing these statues as well as feeding and dressing them. With the water turned to blood, the Egyptians would have been unable to carry out this religious ritual.

Resisting God has a blinding effect, hampering one's ability to employ common sense. We begin to see this with the Egyptian magicians who "did the same things by their secret arts" (v. 22). Did they not see they were only making matters worse? Presumably the clean water they turned to blood was secured by digging along the Nile (see v. 24). Did the folly of their actions never occur to them while digging? Their "power" was enough to convince Pharaoh that Yahweh was no one to fear; did the king not think to have the magicians demonstrate their power by *reversing* the plague? God displayed his miraculous power to Pharaoh, who responded with stubborn pride; the result was a heart increasingly less able to bend, even to common sense.

The second plague took place seven days after the first, a rare chronological reference likely intended to suggest the scope of the first plague. Given that the Nile discharges nearly two hundred fifty million cubic meters of water every day, over the course of a week almost two billion cubic meters of water would have been contaminated in the Nile alone. That is a lot of blood!

God instructed Moses and Aaron to inform the king that unless he allowed the Israelites to go, Egypt would be overrun with frogs. Why frogs? The Egyptians worshiped a goddess known as Heqt, depicted as a woman with the head of a frog. So the plague of frogs may have demonstrated God's power over yet another Egyptian deity. Heqt represented fertility and was married to the ram god, Khnum, who was responsible for fashioning humans from clay, like a potter. Perhaps God was making the point that the Egyptian symbol of fertility and blessing had become a symbol of blight. This possibility is strengthened by the repetition of the verb used to describe the frogs: "teem" (8:3), the same word used to describe the miraculous growth of the Israelites in 1:7. God had at least one more reason for sending frogs: The Egyptians were accustomed to them. An abundance of frogs arrived each year with the flooding of the Nile, an infestation they viewed as a symbol of fertility. Once again, God performed a miracle that could be overlooked as just a coincidence or something the Egyptian magicians could easily do. Yet for those with eyes to see, God left clues that this was indeed a miracle. The frogs arrive precisely when and how God said they would (8:1–6), and they left when he promised they would (vv. 9–13). Actually, they did not leave; they just died and lay rotting in "heaps" (v. 14), a term elsewhere rendered "clay," perhaps another dig at Khnum. Earlier the Egyptians had complained of the stench of the Israelite workmen (see 5:21); now they had a stench of their own making.

Next came the plague of flying insects, variously identified as gnats, lice, or mosquitoes (8:16–19). As with the first two plagues, this phenomenon was not unknown to the Egyptians. Once again, it could easily have been deemed a coincidence. This plague, however, arose not from the water but from the ground. God's subtle message: His power is not limited. The magicians could not replicate this plague, prompting them to warn Pharaoh that this was "the finger of God" (v. 19). How telling it is that the first Egyptians to see what was really happening were those best acquainted with supernatural power.

The second cycle of plagues began with the fourth plague, an infestation of flies (vv. 20–32). Like the other flying insects, the flies arose from the ground. However, in this case the Israelites were spared from the plague (v. 23). God's people endured the effects of the first three plagues, knowing that their suffering was evidence of God's action on their behalf. Though it is not always easy to remember, God's work sometimes causes things to worsen before they get better.

When God made a distinction between the Israelites and Egyptians by sparing Israel the fourth plague, it was an act of mercy to one and a lesson to other. This action made it clear that God was present, concerned about his people, and rising up in their defense. The land became heavy with swarming flies (v. 24). The Hebrew word, here rendered "dense" or "heavy," shows up often in this story. It was used to described Moses' speech impediment (see 4:10), the Israelites' arduous labor (see 5:9), and Pharaoh's heart (see 7:14; 8:15). Describing the flies this way may be a subtle way of emphasizing God's sovereignty. He can avenge the hardship of his people by hardening the heart of the king while employing a stumbling spokesman.

Plague five struck the livestock of only the Egyptians (9:1–7). The reference to the "hand" of God (v. 3) brings to mind God's "finger" in 8:19 and indicates that the situation had become increasingly severe. And so it did. Every horse, donkey, camel, cow, sheep, and goat belonging to the Egyptians died by God's hand through a disease he sent. Some interpret "all" in 9:6 to mean "most" because the Egyptians' livestock were also affected in the next two plagues. Although the term can have that meaning, *all* should probably be taken literally here. The animals later affected had to be purchased from the Israelites, yet another instance of the plundering of the Egyptians. In this case, Pharaoh did not plead for relief as he had following previous plagues. He knew from his investigation that the animals of his people were dead while those of the Israelites were alive. His heart becoming ever harder, Pharaoh refused to yield in spite of the evidence that he should (v. 7).

The second cycle ended with a plague of boils, a festering skin condition that was especially painful and disfiguring (vv. 8–12; see also Lev. 13:18–20, 23; Deut. 28:27, 35; Job 2:7). Oddly, these boils resulted from contact with ashes from a furnace (Ex. 9:10). God may have sent the boils in this way to emphasize the burning pain associated with the boils. Another possibility is that he wanted to connect the plague of boils to a furnace in the minds of the Egyptians and Israelites. The furnace is a commonly used metaphor to describe Israel's experience in Egypt (see Deut. 4:20; 1 Kings 8:51; Jer. 11:4). The association with a furnace may have been even more relevant in this case because bricks were sometimes made using a furnace.[3]

While the magicians replicated the first two plagues, they failed to do so with the third, and they are not even mentioned in the fourth. In the fifth plague, they couldn't appear in Pharaoh's presence because they were afflicted with the boils. Perhaps they stayed away because of their discomfort, or they may have been ashamed at their lack of power to protect or heal themselves. That no mention is made of Pharaoh being stricken may suggest that God spared him, one more way of hardening his heart.

The third cycle of plagues began with a hailstorm unlike any Egypt had seen before (Ex. 9:13–35). As with the first plague in the two preceding cycles, God warned the king through Moses. This time God also announced that from then on he would pull out all the stops. Pharaoh would experience "the full force" (v. 14) of the coming plagues. God made it clear that he could have unleashed this force at the beginning but chose to wait in order to prove that he not Pharaoh, Egypt, or the gods they worshiped possessed all-surpassing power. The great king, perhaps the most powerful man in the world at that time, was a pawn in God's plan to demonstrate his glory to all (v. 16).

Hail is rare in Egypt. This hailstorm was so heavy and accompanied by so much thunder, lightning, and rain that it devastated the crops, trees, and livestock everywhere in Egypt (v. 25)—everywhere except Goshen, home of the Israelites (v. 26).

Moses' confidence was growing. He showed no fear of Pharaoh, courageously rebuking him for fake repentance. Moses even gave the king a theology lesson by referring to the LORD God (*Yahweh Elohim*, v. 30), the only time this combination of divine names is found in Exodus. *Elohim* can function as a proper noun (God), as it does in the title Moses used. It can also be used as an adjective to describing something monumental. Pharaoh used this sense of the word in 9:28 to describe the thunder ("mighty" in KJV; "terrifying" in NLT). Elohim can have a third meaning as a generic noun for gods, of which the Egyptians had hundreds. By using the phrase *Yahweh Elohim*, Moses courageously asserted that the only god the Egyptians needed to fear was Yahweh, God of the Israelites.

With the eighth plague (10:1–20), matters grew even worse for the Egyptians. The few crops that remained after the hailstorm were consumed in a locust plague, which surpassed any Egypt had experienced. The additional descriptive phrase "nor will there ever be again" (v. 14) indicates that this plague was the work of God, the only one capable of making such a prediction.

The locusts were blown in by a wind from the east. Once again God chose to bring this plague using natural means so that those without faith could imagine it as just a nasty coincidence while those who believed would understand the true, divine cause and respond accordingly. Pharaoh's reaction, even against the urging of his own counselors (v. 7), demonstrated how blind he had become.

The ninth plague (10:21–29) cast Egypt into the total, palpable pitch-blackness, like that of a cave or mine. This blackness was more than annoying; it clearly revealed God's power over the most important of the Egyptian gods, the sun god Ra. This catastrophe would have stricken existential terror into the heart of every Egyptian. Their theology held that at sunset Ra passed into the underworld where he was challenged by the monster Apophis. Each sunrise marked the triumph of Ra over the monster. Now Yahweh had caused Ra to disappear and prevented him from reappearing for days on end. More remarkably, the sun continued to shine where the Israelites lived. This was more than an inconvenience; it was a blow at the foundation of Egyptian society.

The conversation that followed between Pharaoh and Moses was the last time the two met face-to-face (10:24—11:8). Before he left, Moses issued a clear warning to Pharaoh of the final, most devastating plague to come, death throughout Egypt. Some Egyptians may have lost their lives during the preceding nine plagues, but human death was never their intent. This final plague, which was to begin that night at midnight, would take the life of every firstborn son in Egypt, from the home of the poorest peasant to the palace of the king himself. Since the firstborn prince was to inherit the mantle of divinity upon becoming the next pharaoh, this plague struck not only at the heart of every parent, but at the pride and stability of Egypt as well. Having delivered his final warning, Moses turned his back on the king and walked out of the palace, fuming with righteous indignation (11:8).

CONCLUSION

By the end of the ninth plague, Egypt had been devastated. A once-great country was in ruins, all except that portion occupied by a group of slaves tracing its ancestry to a man named Abraham. Yet the devastation of Egypt and preservation of Israel was not the purpose of these plagues. We now turn our attention to the reason Yahweh chose to work this way and what part the plagues played in the preparation of God's servants.

5

The Way God Works

Exodus 5–11

The plagues devastated the nation of Egypt, but that was not their primary purpose. God employed this particular strategy of delivering his people for several reasons, weakening Egypt being only one of them. God's greater purpose in using the plagues was to shape the lives of both Pharaoh and Moses. These two men provide a striking contrast in the way they responded to the power and glory of Yahweh. A closer look at Exodus 5–11 will highlight this contrast and help us better understand what makes a faithful servant.

PURPOSES FOR THE PLAGUES

God had multiple options for the method of delivering his people from Egypt. Had he chosen, he could have kept them from becoming slaves in the first place. He could have devastated the land with a single blow, perhaps through an enormous flood that washed away this civilization that clung to the banks of the Nile, or by sending an overpowering invasion by one of Egypt's enemies, or by a deadly virus such as Ebola. Why did God choose to use ten plagues, each one more severe than the last? Why these particular plagues, and why this sequence? Throughout Exodus 5–11, five purposes emerge.

First, God chose this strategy because it had the effect of hardening Pharaoh's heart. The sequence of plagues growing gradually more severe made it easier for Pharaoh to refuse Moses' demand until it was too late. We will return to this point to discuss whether God hardened Pharaoh's heart or Pharaoh hardened his own heart. For now, we see that the hardening of Pharaoh's heart made him less able to realize that his country was being seriously weakened. His heart was eventually so hard he did not even stop to ask what would happen to his army if they rode into the middle of the Red Sea. Though not its primary objective, the plague strategy left Pharaoh with a devastated society and a devastated army. Egypt became too weak to pursue the Israelites, allowing them freedom to remain safe at Sinai for more than a year and in the wilderness for four decades.

A second purpose of the plagues was to demonstrate to the Egyptian people Yahweh's superiority over their gods, as God assured Moses even before the plagues began: "The Egyptians will know that I am the LORD when I stretch out my hand against Egypt and bring the Israelites out of it" (7:5). This national humiliation produced several effects. Once the Egyptians realized their gods were no match for Israel's God, they became "favorably disposed toward the people, and Moses himself was highly regarded in Egypt by Pharaoh's officials and by the people" (11:3). Because the Egyptians feared Yahweh, they also feared Yahweh's people. No doubt some Egyptians were tempted to take revenge on the Israelites for all the devastation in their land, but by enveloping Israel in this divinely induced dread, Yahweh protected his people from personal retaliation. Some Egyptians even abandoned their nation and joined the Israelites. Given the almost fanatical loyalty Egyptians felt toward their country and the disdain they had for all others, this move was truly remarkable.

Those who did not leave felt such high regard for the Israelites that they dug deep in the pockets of their robes to provide a generous send-off. God instructed his people to go to their Egyptian neighbors to ask for silver and gold (v. 2). When they did, they found their neighbors especially generous, a generosity induced by the recognition that these Israelites had a powerful God who might not take kindly to refusal. This was just what God had predicted to Moses, that the Israelites would "plunder the Egyptians" (3:22). At least some of this plunder would be used to build the tabernacle in the wilderness. The bronze basin and its stand were made "from the mirrors of the women who served at the entrance to the tent of meeting" (38:8), mirrors no doubt procured from their Egyptian neighbors. Where else would a group of slaves get almost 2,200 pounds of gold, over 7,500 pounds of silver and over 5,300 pounds of bronze (see vv. 24–25, 29 NLT)?

Third, Yahweh intended the plagues to prove to the Israelites his superiority over the gods of Egypt. In his farewell address, Moses asked the Israelites, "Has any god ever tried to take for himself one nation out of another nation, by testings, by signs and wonders, by war, by a mighty hand and an outstretched arm, or by great and awesome deeds, like all the things the LORD your God did for you in Egypt before your very eyes?" And why did God do this for Israel before their very eyes? "You were shown these things so that you might know that the LORD is God; besides him there is no other" (Deut. 4:34–35).

Imagine yourself as one of those Israelites. Everywhere you looked you saw the grandeur and vibrancy of Egyptian religion. You observed temple after temple filled with magnificent statues of hundreds of gods, elaborate rituals, deeply devoted followers, and doctrines that appeared to explain how life really works. This was all the Israelites had known for generations. For their part, they had no temple, no image of their god, and few, if any, rituals; all they had were stories. Those stories spoke of a future hope, but time and circumstances had weakened that hope to the faintest flicker. What would it take to shatter the centuries-old delusion that Egyptian religion was real and their own was not just empty promises? It would take a celestial smackdown of monumental proportions, one that demonstrated conclusively which god was really all-powerful and which religion real.

God's fourth purpose in using the plague strategy was to create an unforgettable moment that God's people could look back on for years to come. As he explained to Moses just before the plague of locusts, "Go to Pharaoh, for I have hardened his heart and the hearts of his officials so that I may perform these signs of mine among them that you may tell your children and grandchildren how I dealt harshly with the Egyptians and how I performed my signs among them, and that you may know that I am the LORD" (Ex. 10:1–2).

Yahweh wanted this story passed down from generation to generation so future Israelites would know he is the most powerful god and they would not forget they were his people, with all the privileges and responsibilities that accompany that identity. As we will see in the next chapter, God facilitated this memory-making by instituting the festival of Passover at the start of each year as an annual reminder of this event. God's strategy worked, for the exodus became the most significant moment in Israel's collective memory.

Fifth, God chose this method of delivering his people in order to develop their faith. If God had accomplished this deliverance by walloping the Egyptians with a knock-out punch in the first round, the Israelites would have had no trouble believing in God. What other response would be possible after witnessing raw, unmistakable power? But faith developed in that way would have had a short shelf life. Unless God continued to exhibit ever-greater examples of awe-inspiring power, Israel's faith would wither and die.

To develop the faith of his people, God began small, with a miracle even the Egyptian magicians could copy. Recognizing that as an act of Yahweh would have taken faith, but not too much faith. Yet exercising faith in this first miracle would have made it easier to believe in the second. Belief in the second miracle would have made it easier to believe in the third, and so forth. God chose this progressive strategy to develop the Israelites' capacity to believe in him, not for a moment but for a long time.

CONTRASTING REACTIONS: MOSES AND PHARAOH

The way the narrator told this story suggests that we are meant to see Moses and Pharaoh as representing two options for how to respond to God's power. One of these men began holding all the power but became increasingly impotent; the other began with no evident power but turned out to be the unquestioned victor. Faith proven by persistent obedience is what made the difference.

Although Moses' mission began at a burning bush, the flames of that experience quickly diminished. He had not even arrived in Egypt when it looked as if God was trying to kill his appointed deliverer. Moses' initial efforts at bringing deliverance went nowhere; actually, they went backward and left the Israelites worse off than they had been before. All efforts to prove Moses' authority were nullified by the Egyptian magicians. In spite of these setbacks, Moses demonstrated faith by obeying.

Pharaoh possessed all the power and authority one could want. He had every reason to be confident in the Egyptian gods, for they had produced Egypt, the rival of all nations in the ancient Near East and home of building structures that even today, 3,500 years later, inspire admiration. Pharaoh had every reason to be confident in himself. He was not only the most powerful man in that part of the world but also was treated as more than a man, a manifestation of the gods.

From the very beginning, Pharaoh refused to listen to Moses and Aaron. Their little miracles proved nothing, and the first two plagues may have been nothing more than coincidences. With each decision to disbelieve, Pharaoh grew more resolved to continue on that path. Even as the evidence grew, his accumulating denial inoculated him against a change of mind. The less he believed, the less he was able to believe.

Readers of Exodus have long puzzled over who hardened Pharaoh's heart. At times we read that Pharaoh's heart had become hard and unyielding (7:13–14, 22; 8:19; 9:7, 35). In other passages, God is said to have hardened the king's heart (4:21; 7:3; 9:12; 10:1, 20, 27; 11:10; 14:4, 8, 17); in still others, Pharaoh hardened his own heart (8:15, 32; 9:34). All are accurate descriptions of what took place. God intentionally created a scenario in which Pharaoh's own pride and stubbornness combined to harden the king's heart. The king's heart became hard both as the result of his choices and by God's intent and design.

The hardening of the human heart works much like strong adhesives known as epoxies. Epoxies are stored in two separate containers, one holding the resin, the other the hardener. The two liquids can sit alongside one another on a shelf for months with no result. Only when the elements are combined does the hardening occur. God does not force his will; he does not need to. He need only provide the right conditions to allow the heart to progress in the direction it naturally leans. When it came to Pharaoh, God provided the right conditions, knowing Pharaoh would willingly do the rest.

One of those conditions was a challenge to the king's pride and power. The challenge began in a small way, with a miracle just slightly more powerful than his magicians could copy. A humble man would have acknowledged he had been beaten, but not the mighty king of Egypt. Each proud refusal invited another challenge, more serious than the last. The Egyptian magicians were beaten, afflicted with boils they could not remove. Then the Egyptian gods were beaten. Later, as Pharaoh watched his army sink beneath the waves of the Red Sea, he himself was beaten. Pharaoh hardened his own heart by persistently refusing to humble himself before the greater power. God hardened Pharaoh's heart by providing the right conditions for that to happen.

God also hardened Pharaoh's heart, and the hearts of many others, by creating the moral universe we occupy. In this universe, repeated choices, freely made, produce consequences. We are free to make the choices but not free to choose which consequences accompany them. The content of our thoughts significantly shapes the choices we make. Pharaoh's self-exalting thoughts made it more likely that he would reject God's demands. He was free to choose otherwise, but he would have had to go against his own thoughts. Repeated choices form a habit. Pharaoh's initial rejection of God led to a habit of rejecting him. Habitual behavior signifies character. Character shapes destiny, which, for the once-proud Egyptian monarch, was the devastation of his nation and his own disgrace. God hardened Pharaoh's heart not by forcing Pharaoh to choose against his will but by designing a moral universe where freely chosen actions eventuate in destiny.

When this story began, Pharaoh was the most powerful man in his world. With each decision to disbelieve, Pharaoh grew weaker

MOSES: FAITHFUL SERVANT OF GOD

until, by the end, he could only stand by helpless as the Red Sea swallowed his mighty army. By contrast, Moses grew more confident with each plague. His confidence was not in himself but in the God he served. By the third plague, Moses even allowed Pharaoh to set the time the plague would end (8:9). The fifth and sixth plagues (flies, livestock) arrived without Moses and Aaron lifting a finger. All they had to do was speak the word and the disasters fell. Moses knew when the flies would depart and announced it a day in advance (8:29). When he asked God to remove the flies, it was not with desperate cries, as with the plague of frogs, but only in prayer (v. 29).

At first Moses needed his brother as spokesman, but by the end, Moses did all the talking. At first Moses complained to God about Pharaoh's refusals (5:22-23), but by the end, Moses refused to bend to Pharaoh's proposed compromise (10:25-26). At first Moses spoke to Pharaoh with timidity (5:3), but by the end, God's servant was in control of the conversation, issuing ominous warnings, rebukes, and pronouncements to the king (9:2-4, 13-19, 29-30; 10:1-6; 11:4-8). At first Moses and Aaron were ignored and excluded from Pharaoh's deliberations with the Israelite leaders (5:20), but by the end, it was Moses who, recognizing the futility of future meetings, announced to Pharaoh that they would never again meet face-to-face (10:29).

How does someone go from offering one lame excuse after another for his inability to trust God to having the courage to confront a king? How is the most powerful man in the world confined to a prison of his own construction while a fugitive shepherd with a speech impediment is poised to free an entire people? One believed God and the other didn't. One chose to believe what he had always known and what his culture reinforced while the other was willing to accept God's version of the events and hope for something altogether new. One limited his trust to only those things that seemed reasonable, while the other knew reason to be God's servant not God's master.

Because Moses believed God, he was able to step out in obedience. It was not enough to believe God had called him. Nor was it enough to believe God could deliver through powerful plagues. Moses had to demonstrate his faith through obedience. That was not easy. It required Moses to face off against raw power with only the invisible hand of God for support. Against Egypt's great civilization with deities around every corner, Moses trusted his Master more than his own senses, more than his reason, even more than his experiences.

God was gracious enough to make the first step an easy one, but Moses still had to take it. Once he did, he found the courage for the second step. Each succeeding step was built on the faith shown earlier, like an ascending staircase. Pharaoh built a stairway as well, only his went down. Initial disbelief, fostered by pride, led to Pharoah's disobedience. That disobedience made it more likely he would step down again and again and again until he found himself at the bottom of the stairway, too weak to ascend.

Faith makes all the difference but not merely faith in God's sovereign power. The demons believe in God's sovereign power and tremble, but such faith does not do them any good (see James 2:19). If Moses had had faith only in God's sovereign power, he would not have been able to deliver his people. He would not have been a faithful servant of God. Moses also had faith that God's sovereign power would work through him. That's what made the difference.

God loves to exercise his power through human beings. Whether called divine-human synergy or, as John Wesley described it, "co-operant grace," God works through partnership. Of course, we would be totally unsuitable partners apart from God's grace. Those who are "dead in [their] transgressions and sins" (Eph. 2:1) can offer little assistance to anyone. But those who receive God's grace become responsible to use it by cooperating with what God is doing. God does many things in our lives that we cannot do, but those things are not likely to happen unless we do what we must do.

The distribution of labor in this partnership is unequal. God's load is a lot heavier than ours. God delivered the ten plagues. All Moses had to do was talk, raise his arms, and toss ashes into the air. But because Moses did his part, God's powerful plagues became even more useful to God's purposes. Without Moses' involvement, the plagues would have been seen as inexplicable catastrophes. With Moses' involvement, the plagues could be clearly seen as Yahweh's campaign against Israel's oppressors. God could have spoken directly to Pharaoh without Moses' help. But because he did not confirms the point that God could have done this without Moses but prefers to work in partnership with his people.

Divine-human synergy would come into play many times for God's servant in the days and months to come. God would lead the people so that their backs were up against the Red Sea, then Moses would have to do his part to divide the waters. God would deliver the law to Moses, but he would have to carry the tablets down the mountain and teach the commandments to the people. God would lead the people to a place in the wilderness where water could be found, but Moses would need to strike the rock to bring it forth. God would provide manna for the people, but Moses would have to explain how to gather it.

Remembering that this mission involved divine-human synergy helped Moses remain obedient. It also prevented him from thinking he was totally responsible. The one occasion when he forgot that and struck the rock rather than speaking to it as God had instructed turned out badly for Moses (Num. 20:11–12). The burden of leading

God's people was bearable only because Moses knew he was not the only one carrying it (see Num. 11:14).

Recognizing that he was in a partnership, albeit an unequal one, and faithfully carrying his end of the load made Moses a faithful servant of God. This is what it means to be a servant, to be in partnership with the Master. The Master does what only he can do, enabling the servant to do what the servant should do.

CONCLUSION

God is sovereign but often chooses to exercise that sovereignty in league with us. We cannot do his part, and he will not do ours. When we each do our own part, God accomplishes his perfect plan. God could have chosen an easier way to accomplish that plan, but then faith would be unnecessary. We would be ill-equipped to be God's faithful servants.

God's power in partnership with Moses' faithfulness brought the mighty Egyptians to their knees. However, one final blow remained before the nation fell, and God ensured that its full force would fall only on the Egyptians and that his people would grasp the full significance of what happened. The next chapter considers how God finalized the deliverance of the Israelites and what those events teach us about being faithful servants of God.

6

Moses and the Passover

Exodus 12:1—15:21

After serving as God's junior partner in the destruction of Egypt, Moses' role changed dramatically in Exodus 12. Although he continued to represent God to the people, Moses began to address the Israelite leaders and people rather than Pharaoh. He spent most of the next several chapters helping the people understand how to prepare for the events to come and how to ensure they would always remember the incredible event that was about to happen.

GOD'S TRIPLE DELIVERANCE

Egypt had been devastated by the nine plagues, but Pharaoh remained unbending. His defiance had grown more stubborn even as his country crumbled around him. Yet before the Israelites could be liberated, God would administer one final blow, the death of the firstborn.

This blow did not fall without warning. Before his final meeting with Pharaoh, Moses told the king that at midnight Yahweh would "pass through Egypt and strike down every firstborn of both people and animals" (Ex. 12:12). No household would be exempt, from the barn to the dungeon to the lowliest hovel and all the way to the king's palace (v. 29).

God likely chose this as the final stroke for several reasons. First, the firstborn animal was considered particularly valuable, possessing the qualities of that animal in exceptional measure (see Deut. 33:17). So too, the firstborn son represented the "first sign of his father's strength" (Deut. 21:17; see also Ps. 105:36). As the principal hope of each family, firstborn sons were honored above all other children. To have the entire society bereft of firstborn sons would be a national crisis.

A second reason for targeting the firstborn sons of Egypt was to exact punishment for how Egypt had treated Israel, specifically identified as God's firstborn son. Moses was instructed to warn Pharaoh to release God's firstborn or else God would "kill your firstborn son" (Ex. 4:22–23).

Third, by sparing the firstborn of Israel's sons and livestock, God demonstrated his right to claim these as his own. Because "the LORD killed the firstborn of both people and animals in Egypt," the Israelites were to "sacrifice to the LORD the first male offspring of every womb and redeem each of [their] firstborn sons" (13:15; see also Num. 3:13).

Fourth, the death of Egypt's firstborn was a judgment on Egypt's gods (see Ex. 12:12; Num. 33:4). The death of the crown prince meant a break in the line of succession, a particular threat considering the Egyptians viewed their monarch as the manifestation of a god. The devastation of society brought about through this plague demonstrated the impotence of the Egyptian gods, who were unable to protect their own people.

This plague was described as coming directly from God's hand to a greater degree than the others had been. Note the emphasis on what God will do: "I will go throughout Egypt" (Ex. 11:4); "I will pass through Egypt and strike down every firstborn . . . I will bring judgment on all the gods of Egypt. . . . When I see the blood, I will pass over you . . . when I strike Egypt" (12:12–13); "When the LORD goes through the land to strike down the Egyptians, he will see the blood . . . and will pass over" (v. 23).

Two passages in Exodus suggest that God was not alone on his midnight mission. In Exodus 12:23, we learn that he was accompanied by a "destroyer," who carried out God's direction. The same term is used in verse 13 (without the definite article), where the New International Version renders it "destructive plague." We read this term several more times in the Old Testament. It may describe humans (see 1 Sam. 13:17) or angels, such as the one sent to punish the city of Jerusalem after David's sinful census (see 2 Sam. 24:16). The psalmist understood this tenth plague to be accomplished by not one but by "a detachment of destroying angels" (Ps. 78:49 NJB). By describing this final blast as something God did directly, the narrator emphasized God's power and sovereignty. By describing this as something done by one or more of God's deputies, the narrator highlighted God's dignity.

Once the blow fell, the Israelites were free to leave Egypt. They did so in haste, passing by the Egyptians, who were engaged in the agonizing task of burying their sons (see Num. 33:3–4). But they were not yet truly free, not so long as the Egyptian army could pursue and recapture them. This fearful possibility would haunt them long after they left Egyptian soil. They would be vulnerable as they journeyed to Canaan and even after they arrived there, for they would still be close enough for Egypt to exact a devastating revenge. Only if the Egyptian army were severely crippled would the Israelites be truly free from the threat of retaliation. This, too, was part of God's deliverance of his people.

Centuries of delay ended in an instant as the command to go spread among the Israelites from house to house. In haste they collected their belongings, even their unbaked bread, and traveled from Rameses southeast to Sukkoth (Ex. 12:37). From there they likely expected to head northeast along the coast of the Mediterranean Sea. This was the Way of the Sea (sometimes called the Way of Horus), the quickest way from Egypt to Canaan. So when the order came to "turn back and encamp near Pi Hahiroth" (14:2), the Israelites must have thought there had been some mistake. Yes, they were following Yahweh's pillar of fire and cloud, but this route would delay their departure from Egyptian soil and place them in a vulnerable location, trapped with their backs to the Yam Suph (see 13:21).

Although usually rendered Red Sea, Yam Suph is a Hebrew term and likely refers instead to the Reed Sea, located north of the Gulf of Suez in the territory now divided by the Suez Canal. In ancient times, this region contained freshwater lakes large enough to support commercial shipping.[1] God identified at least two reasons for leading them along this route. First, it would allow the Israelites to avoid encountering the string of Egyptian forts that dotted the Way of Horus, beginning with the Egyptian fortress, Tjaru. Second, it would lead Pharaoh to think the Israelites were "wandering around the land in confusion" (14:3). He might assume the God who had delivered the Israelites did not know how to lead them out of Egypt or this Yahweh had abandoned them. Either way, Pharaoh concluded that the Israelites were now ripe for the picking. God likely had additional reasons other than the two stated. He wanted to eliminate the Egyptian army as a threat to the Israelites, and he wanted to teach what it meant to be his faithful servants.

MOSES AND THE PASSOVER

When the Israelites realized Pharaoh was pursuing them with the Egyptian army, they panicked. Just a short while before, they had witnessed God's mighty power in delivering them from captivity, but now they could muster up only despairing complaints. At least Moses kept his head, though he was facing the wrong direction. He likely expected God to destroy the Egyptian army; he may even have been praying or "crying out" (v. 15) for that. But God had another plan, one that would require Moses to turn around and face the sea. In that direction lay both the path to deliverance and the destruction of the Egyptian army.

God could have parted the sea in an instant, but instead he chose to use a strong east wind that blew all night. In the predawn darkness, illuminated by the pillar of fire, the Israelites began to cross the dry seabed. Pharaoh soon realized the Israelites were escaping across what had been, just yesterday, an impassable sea. He issued the order to advance, and the chariots began their pursuit between the walls of water. "During the last watch of the night," that is, just as light was dawning, God "threw [the Egyptian army] into confusion" (v. 24). Chariot wheels began to come loose, jam, or bog down in the mud. In the midst of their confusion, the army was struck with the blinding realization that they were trapped. Israel's God had lured them into the sea to drown them. They turned around and began to race toward the shore from which they had come. At just that moment, God instructed Moses to once again extend his hand over the sea and collapse the walls of waters to drown the Egyptian army. Safely on the opposite shore, the Israelites saw with their own eyes that God had not only allowed them to leave Egypt but also delivered them from the Egyptian army. Rather than fear the Egyptians, they feared Yahweh and trusted his servant, Moses.

This was a double deliverance, two episodes that parallel one another. In the first, God's angel was the means of destruction

(12:23); in the second, the angel was the means of protection (14:19). In the first, God instructed his people to stay put in their houses (12:22); in the second, they were told to move on (14:15). Destruction passed over them in the first deliverance (12:23), while they passed through the destruction in the second (14:21–23). Israel marched out like a mighty army after the first deliverance, indicated by the repeated reference to Israel leaving in divisions (6:26; 7:4; 12:17, 41, 51). The second deliverance saw the total destruction of the opposing army (14:28). The first deliverance meant freedom from bondage; the second meant freedom from fear.

God accomplished a third act of deliverance in these chapters, less dramatic but far more lasting. Even before the tenth plague, God ordered Moses to instruct the people how to commemorate that fateful night. Those instructions are detailed in Exodus 12 and the first part of chapter 13. God began by providing directions for the first Passover meal, then details on the plague itself. Only after the Israelite elders had been taught how to observe the first Passover meal and future Passovers did the tenth plague occur, followed by Israel's departure from Egypt. The account of the departure is interrupted for a few more instructions on the Passover and directions for setting apart Israel's firstborn males—both human and animal— for God's use. The narrator related the details in this way partly to heighten the suspense but more so to emphasize that God intended the events surrounding this deliverance to become a permanent part of Israel's national memory.

According to God's design, the first Passover meal marked a new beginning, a break with the long and sorry chapter of Israel's slavery in Egypt. Their deliverance had not yet taken place; God instructed them to celebrate that deliverance in advance. A day—what would have been just an ordinary day of servitude—was designated as the first of the month of Abib, the first day of Israel's new existence.

MOSES AND THE PASSOVER

What changed on that day? Nothing changed. They remained slaves of the Egyptians. To the rest of Egypt, this was just another day on the calendar. Yet everything changed, for on the first of Abib the Israelites became a new people with a new destiny. They were assigned a task: to count off ten days. They must have felt a bit like those future Israelites whose battle strategy against Jericho was to march once around the city, then return to camp. Is that it? Yes, that's it. God's servants—Moses and the Israelites—had to understand that God's timing is not theirs; their work was simply to trust.

After counting ten days, the Israelites were to select a lamb or goat. It had to be one year old, without defect, and large enough to feed the household (12:3, 5). For slaves, this was a sacrifice. Clearly, freedom would not be free. They were instructed to care for the animal for four days. This could mean that they were to treat it with special kindness but more likely means they were to watch over it closely to ensure that nothing happened to it. The four-day period helped the Israelites understand the significance of what was about to happen. This animal, the object of their careful attention for several days, would be killed, its life the means of delivering theirs. All these animals would be slaughtered on the same day and at the same time, twilight.

The blood of that lamb or goat was smeared on the "sides and tops of the doorframes" of each Israelite house (v. 7) using hyssop, a common plant (probably Syrian marjoram), whose leaves functioned as a paint brush. The bloodstains were not for God's benefit; he already knew where his people lived. The stains would serve as a visible reminder to Israel of the reason they were spared. The bloodstains would protect them only if they remained inside their homes. The stains would also stand as mute testimony to the Egyptians, who knew that the blood made the difference between life and death.

Inside the house, the animal was to be carefully roasted. It was not to be eaten raw—they were not in that much of a hurry. Nor was it to be boiled, presumably because that would have required breaking the animal's bones (v. 46). Also on the menu were bitter herbs. The bread for the meal was to be made without yeast. They were to eat all the meat, leaving nothing until morning. Imagine every Israelite getting up from the table that night feeling the same as you do after a Thanksgiving Day meal. Indeed, this meal marked a moment of great celebration.

However, they were still slaves in Egypt when they sat down to supper. They ate in anticipation of imminent deliverance; even their wardrobe indicated they were about to head out on a journey. An Egyptian peeking through the window that night would have had quite a laugh seeing feasting Israelite slaves dressed to travel. But the next morning would reveal a different story: an empty house with bloodstains on the doorposts, the occupants well on their way to freedom. God taught Moses and the Israelites the importance of living by faith rather than by sight. They were no longer to reckon the present and future as the unbroken result of the past. They were now to count time by God's calendar and define themselves on God's terms.

The Passover meal itself was part of God's lesson. He meant for the Israelites to increase in understanding with every bite. Deliverance would come from God's hands, but they would have to be personally involved, willing to pay the price, and fully attentive to the required details. All Israelites would be required to participate, but certain non-Israelites could as well, so long as they were circumcised (vv. 44–45, 48), an anticipation of Israel's role in blessing all nations (vv. 44–48). Israel's bitter servitude was ending, consumed by God as easily as they ate their strong greens. Their flatbread testified to the suddenness of deliverance, so sudden there was not even time for the bread to rise. God delivered his people, and he delivered a message to them, one that would be repeated and reinforced for centuries, sustaining them in their darkest moments.

Through the rituals of Passover, the Israelites experienced their deliverance even before it came about. In a similar way, God calls his people today to walk by faith. We are to celebrate the deliverance brought to us by the Lamb of God while waiting for the fullness of that deliverance—complete reconciliation with God, one another, ourselves, and nature. We anticipate that deliverance through the bread and cup of the Lord's Supper, fully cognizant of the cost of Christ's sacrifice and the freedom it brings. Whether we come to the Lord's Table in our Sunday best or something more casual, we know that these are traveling clothes, for we are awaiting the signal to begin the ultimate journey to our true home, the new heaven and new earth.

To ensure the permanence of this memory of deliverance, God told Moses to instruct the Israelites to celebrate Passover annually. It was to be the first day of a week-long celebration, the Festival of Unleavened Bread (vv. 14–20), so called because the Israelites were not to consume anything containing yeast during that time. Flatbread had been a matter of necessity for the first Passover because their departure from Egypt happened so fast they did not have time for dough to rise. In the future, they would celebrate the suddenness of that deliverance for seven days; flatbread meant freedom. The absence of yeast also meant ready obedience, since it implied the need to leave as soon as God opened the door. This celebration was to be a reminder of the necessity of faith.

The first and last days of this festival were for sacred assembly, that is, days when Israel was to do nothing but rest and enjoy what God had given. Imagine how this must have sounded to a nation of slaves. After years of backbreaking forced labor, finally rest. Rest implies the freedom to choose how to spend one's time. Instructions to celebrate this in perpetuity meant perpetual freedom.

In Exodus 12:24–28, God explained that he established this lasting memorial so his people would never forget that he had delivered them. Remembering this would help them remember who they were: God's people who had been chosen for a divine purpose, to bring about the fullness of God's redemptive plan. Remembering their past deliverance would also remind them of God's faithful love, filling them with gratitude and making it easier to trust God for future needs. These verses describe a triple deliverance: from bondage in Egypt, from fear of reprisal, and from forgetfulness.

This was not to be the only ongoing reminder of deliverance for the Israelites. Because God had passed over the Israelites, sparing every firstborn son and male domestic animal among them, God claimed every firstborn male for his own from this point forward (13:1–16). In fact, every person and animal among the Israelites belonged to God. All owed their origin to the moment God called Abraham from Ur; all owed their freedom to the deliverance God wrought through the plagues. God demanded the firstborn to reinforce his rightful supremacy and to remind them of this singular moment of deliverance. God also instructed the Israelites to explain the reason for this claim to their children. When children asked what it meant that the firstborn son must be redeemed at a price and the firstborn of the animals sacrificed or redeemed, they were to explain, "With a mighty hand the Lord brought us out of Egypt, out of the land of slavery. When Pharaoh stubbornly refused to let us go, the Lord killed the firstborn of both people and animals in Egypt. This is why I sacrifice to the Lord the first male offspring of every womb and redeem each of my firstborn sons" (vv. 14–15). The commemoration of Passover and the Feast of Unleavened Bread would be "like a sign on [their] hand and a symbol on [their] forehead" (vv. 9, 16), a reminder to them and a reminder to others. Clearly, God did not want his people to forget what he had done for them and why.

MOSES AND THE PASSOVER

LESSONS FOR A SERVANT

Our God knows how to multitask, for while he delivered his people from centuries of slavery, he also taught his people, especially his chief servant, Moses, several important lessons. First, God demonstrated his incredible power over all that would or could oppose him. One of the most powerful humans in the world, the Egyptian pharaoh, was forced to look on, impotent, as his elite forces laid dead on the shore. Behind him stretched his country, also devastated by Yahweh's powerful arm. And nature could not stand in God's way either, as proven by the increasingly devastating plagues. The Nile River, dust, sky, livestock, sun, and sea—nature bent to the force of God's sovereign will as easily as clay to the hands of a potter.

This was also a supernatural conflict, a celestial smackdown. Those involved in this conflict understood that it went beyond the two peoples; it was a contest between their gods. None of the Egyptian gods could protect their people from Yahweh, not even the most-high sun god, Ra. We now understand that behind the Egyptian gods lay the embodiment of evil whose name we know as Satan. The archfiend suffered a devastating blow at Israel's deliverance but returned to fight another day.

Both the Egyptians and Israelites would also have recognized a third level to this conflict. Beyond the conflict between peoples and the underlying contest between their gods were certain assumptions about the world. Scholars use the term *myth* to describe this level of thinking. These are not make-believe stories told to entertain children. Myths are stories that answer the fundamental questions people ask about their existence, such as: What is a human being? Where did we come from? Why do we exist? What has value? How can we be happy? What is our greatest fear?

The greatest fear in the ancient Near East—the fear that kept Egyptians and Israelites awake at night—was that the orderly world upon which they depended would be swallowed up by chaos. The cultures of the ancient Near East shared this fear, and they shared the symbols for order and chaos: mountains and sea, respectively. When God parted the waters of the Red Sea, he opened a way for the Israelites to escape, destroyed the Egyptian army, and demonstrated his power over nature. And he did something more: He proved he controlled the fundamental source of fear, the sea. The Old Testament echoes this testimony of God's power over chaos. The creation account describes God establishing order out of what was "formless and empty" with God's Spirit "hovering over the waters" (Gen. 1:2). The psalmist confidently asserted that even if "the earth [gave] way and the mountains [fell] into the heart of the sea," we would have no need to fear (Ps. 46:2). The psalmist made this claim while alluding to the events at the Red Sea (see 74:13; 77:16, 19). Not only is Yahweh greater than the Egyptian gods, but his power is absolute.

A second lesson God taught Moses and the Israelites was that God intended to exercise his power through a divine-human partnership. He would pass through the land of Egypt and kill the firstborn, but Moses had to pass along instructions about how to survive to the Israelites. The Israelites also had a role to play: choosing then slaughtering an animal, placing its blood on the doorposts, and preparing a meal with a specific menu. God would lead them out of Egypt, but they would need to follow. God would eliminate any need to fear the pursuing Egyptian army, but Moses would need to stretch out his hand over the waters, and the Israelites would need to enter the watery chasm, flanked on either side by liquid walls. God would do his part, but he would *not* do theirs. Success depended on all doing their part.

A third lesson God taught was that the Israelites should never forget what happened while they were leaving Egypt. He wanted their deliverance from Egypt to become a permanent memory in their collective consciousness, shaping how they understood themselves. He wanted them to recall that they had been slaves but were liberated by their God. He wanted them to remember that they had been graciously chosen and made God's partners in an eternal covenant. He wanted them never to forget that all they had came from him, a gift from their generous Liberator. This memory would help them trust God in times of difficulty or threat. To know they had been chosen as God's partners not because of what they had to offer but by God's grace gave them the confidence and courage to trust him.

The Israelites needed to remember this not only for their own sake but also for the sake of those who would come after. Their own children would need to know (Ex. 12:26), as would Israelites for generations to come. What had happened at the exodus would be just as relevant for future generations as for those who actually walked between the watery walls.

Because the Israelites did not forget, those living more than a millennia later were able to see the connections between these events and the life and ministry of Jesus. They recognized the similarities between the Passover and Christ's death. Paul could write to the Corinthians, "Get rid of the old yeast, so that you may be a new unleavened batch—as you really are. For Christ, our Passover lamb, has been sacrificed" (1 Cor. 5:7). Centuries later, Saint Augustine, in one of his homilies on John's gospel, spoke of how that "prophetic emblem [was] fulfilled in truth, when Christ [was] led as a sheep to the slaughter, that by his blood sprinkled on our doorposts, that is, by the sign of his cross marked on our foreheads, we may be delivered from the perdition awaiting this world, as Israel [was delivered] from the bondage and destruction of the Egyptians."[2]

These and other authors understood that the exodus represented a deliverance far greater even than from the hands of the Egyptians. Through Christ, our Passover Lamb, God delivered not only the Israelites but also the people of every nation, tribe, and tongue. Even this is hinted at in the account of the exodus, where we read that "many other people went up with" the Israelites, likely Egyptians who became convinced of the superiority of Yahweh over their own gods (Ex. 12:38).

The deliverance in this greater exodus was not from Egyptian slavery but from bondage to sin. During the exodus, nature once again became an ally as the waters parted to allow the Israelites to escape, then closed to swallow the pursuing enemy. In the greater deliverance, the curse will be lifted entirely (Rev. 22:3) and nature will finally and forever become humanity's friend.

The beneficiaries of this greater deliverance also are responsible to remember. We, too, have rituals, baptism and the Lord's Supper, through which we commemorate our freedom in Christ and the powerful divine acts that made our freedom possible. We remember for our own sakes and for the sake of those who will follow us.

These three lessons were to be learned by God's servants, who were to pass them along to future generations. Moses was responsible to instruct the elders, who would instruct others (Ex. 12:21). These lessons would then be passed down from one generation to another so all would remember. God's servants serve him by serving others, including those who come long after. Moses may not have fully understood the significance of what he and the Israelites experienced in their deliverance from Egypt, but God's servants must faithfully carry out their roles even when they do not fully understand what God is doing through them.

CONCLUSION

In the exodus, God freed the Israelites from Egyptian bondage. Before they could enter the land he had promised, however, they needed to experience yet another liberation. Here again, Moses would play a pivotal role in this deeper act of deliverance and would learn important lessons about what it means to be God's faithful servant.

The Servant in the Wilderness

Exodus 15:22—18:27; Numbers 20

God wanted to do more than simply get his people out of Egypt and into Canaan. Had that been the only item on his to-do list, he could have done it quickly and powerfully. The Israelites could have been on their way up the Mediterranean coast and in the Promised Land within a matter of weeks. Yet instead of leading the people on the more direct northeastern route to Canaan, God steered them southeast, toward Sinai. Before they could experience the fullness of his plan for them, they would have to learn what it meant to be his people. Although Moses had learned much in the school of servanthood, he, too, had more lessons to learn, lessons only the wilderness could teach.

THE MASTER PROVIDES

One of the lessons God's servants would learn was that he provides. The wilderness was a perfect place to teach this lesson, for this land was desolate, bereft of the provisions needed for a large group of people. That is why so many of the crises in these chapters concern water and food.

Some questions remain about how large of a group actually left Egypt. High estimates place the number at two million to three million, calculated by taking the number of fighting men, stated as about six hundred thousand (see Ex. 12:37; 38:26; Num. 1:46), and extrapolating the number of women and children. This fits the claim of Israel's supernaturally rapid growth and the fear the Egyptians felt toward them (Ex. 1:7, 9–10, 20).

Other scholars propose a much smaller number, perhaps as few as twenty thousand to twenty-five thousand. They point out that this still constitutes a rapid growth rate but better fits the biblical and archaeological evidence. For example, archaeologists estimate the Egyptian army to have been around twenty-five thousand at that time. Even with their chariots, they would have been no match for an Israelite army of six hundred thousand, yet the Israelites cowered in fear when confronted by their enemy (14:10). Evidence suggests that the total population of Canaan was between fifty thousand and one hundred fifty thousand when the Israelites arrived.[1] Yet Exodus 23:30 describes Israel as too small in number to take over the entire land at once, and Deuteronomy 7:7 refers to Israel as "the smallest of all nations" (NLT). How does one account for the statement that the Israelite army numbered six hundred thousand? Some scholars have suggested that the word usually rendered "thousand" was meant to be translated as "clan" or "military unit" (see 1 Sam. 10:19). Others have suggested treating this number as hyperbolic or symbolic. "Numbers in the biblical world," writes one conservative scholar, "often have more sophisticated vocations than counting."[2] However this issue is decided, catering for this expedition in the wilderness required a miracle. Regardless of whether there were twenty thousand or three million Israelites, there was not enough food and water to keep them alive.

The lack of food and water became apparent after only three days (Ex. 15:22–27). The water the Israelites had brought with them when they left Egypt was running out, and they had found no source of water from which they could resupply. Their hopes rose when they spotted water only to sink even lower when they found it was too bitter to drink. Some scholars have suggested the problem with that water source was that it contained too much magnesium sulfate.[3] Whatever the reason, finding undrinkable water was worse than finding none at all. Naturally, the Israelites complained to Moses. He was, after all, their leader. But Moses understood that he was only God's servant; this expedition and its route were God's idea, so God would have to solve this problem.

God pointed out to Moses a particular tree that he was to throw into the waters. When Moses did so, the water became drinkable (v. 25). Similar miracles later in Israel's history include Elisha throwing salt into undrinkable water adding meal or flour to poisonous stew, and throwing a stick into the Jordan to make the lost axe head float (2 Kings 2:19–22; 4:38–41; 6:1–7). The connection between the object involved and the positive outcome it produced is as much a mystery in the exodus incident as in the others. Beyond healing the waters, God used this occasion to teach something to Moses and the Israelites: God could heal them as easily as he healed these waters, if they would only trust and obey. To emphasize his point, God then led them to an oasis with plenty of water, where they set up camp (Ex. 15:25–27).

Around this same time, the Israelites began to grumble about the shortage of food (16:1–3), likely because they had exhausted the supplies they had brought with them from Egypt. The question of resupplying in this barren land loomed in their minds. Yes, God could lead them to water, but how could he lead them to enough food? Unable to see good options before them, the Israelites began to look behind them, back to Egypt. There, they fantasized, they had all they could eat, even all the meat they wanted. In despair, they imagined that they would have been better off if only they had died in the plagues along with the Egyptians because, they thought, God had intentionally brought them to the desert to starve to death. Their distorted view of the past, present, and future as well as their abject despair, coming before two months had passed since the parting of the Red Sea and mere days from the miracle at Elim, seems impossible. That is, until we examine our own lives and consider how quickly we, too, have forgotten God's recent manifestations of goodness and begun to lose hope.

God had many options for providing sufficient food. He could have led them by a different, less desolate route. He could have miraculously replenished their existing supplies, as he did with the widow's oil and grain, or he could have enlisted thousands of ravens to deliver food daily, as he did with Elijah (1 Kings 17:1–16). He could even have temporarily taken away their need for food. He chose, instead, to deliver through the daily supply of a food called manna.

The Israelites had no idea what this new foodstuff was, which is why they named it manna, Hebrew for "What is it?" It may have been a naturally occurring substance, such as the excretions of scale insects and plant lice that live in trees and shrubs and ingest flower clusters and excrete the sap. If not harvested by morning, other insects would remove it. The excretions could have been gathered during the months of May, June, and July.[4] Or it may have been something entirely new and never seen before, miraculously invented by God for this purpose. Either way, it was a miracle. Whether God invented it at that moment or miraculously multiplied a naturally occurring substance, the miracle was not *what* God provided but *how*.

We should not be surprised by this, given how many of the plagues could be explained as phenomena of nature. Even the parting of the Red Sea is explained in the Bible itself as the result of a strong east wind. God chose to provide food in this way to impress upon his people the need to recognize his hand in what others might regard as merely a natural event or coincidence.

The Israelites would demonstrate their awareness that this was a miracle of divine provision by following God's directions for gathering and preserving the manna. Each Sunday through Thursday, the people were to collect enough food for each member of the household for that day only. On Friday they were to collect double the amount. On the Sabbath, they were not to go out, for they would find nothing there. This was to be a day of rest; God would provide a double ration for them on Friday. Naturally, some tested these boundaries looking for a better way, but they failed. Hoarding produced only rotten manna; obedience meant fresh manna, even on the Sabbath.

And there was more. God provided meat, a luxury in the ancient Near East. One wonders if his decision to add meat to the menu may have had something to do with the Israelites' claim—likely bogus—that they had sat around pots of meat in Egypt (Ex. 16:3). In place of make-believe meat, God provided the real thing.

Here again, God used a naturally occurring phenomenon to accomplish the miracle. Annually, flocks of quail fly across this stretch of land. In the spring they travel west to east across the Gulf of Sinai, reversing course in the fall. In both seasons the quail must fly across large stretches of open water, leaving them exhausted by the time they reach land. The miracle was the timing and scope of the birds' arrival, which were just as God had promised. While the manna lasted until the Israelites reached Canaan, the supply of quail was likely limited in duration.[5]

As the Israelites approached Mount Sinai, they once again ran short on water with no supply in sight (17:1–7). Again they complained to Moses—this time with greater animosity and perhaps veiled threats of bodily harm (v. 4)—and once again Moses turned to God. This time God provided a different solution. He instructed Moses to take a group of elders and move ahead of the people to the foot of Mount Sinai (Horeb), where he was told to strike a certain rock with his staff. When Moses did so, water gushed out.

Once again, God did more than perform a miracle. Class was in session for Moses, the elders, and the people of Israel. The staff employed was specifically identified as Moses' staff, the one with which he had initiated the first plague. The same God who had delivered them from Egypt would be the one who provided for them in the desert. God would use the same human leader, Moses, now as he had then. Moses was to take the elders with him to serve as witnesses of the miraculous way God led Moses to the rock and provided the water. It would be their responsibility to share this information, fostering faithfulness in the people they led.

Moses and the elders were to move ahead of the rest of the Israelites. This demonstrated that the people would have reached a water supply in a short time if they had only been patient. How many times do we give up too soon, imagining all hope is gone, when, if we had been willing to hold out for just a little while longer, we would have seen God's miraculous provision?

God informed Moses that he would "stand there before" Moses (v. 6), presumably identifying the particular spot where Moses was to strike the rock. We are not told how Moses would know where the invisible God was standing; it may have been either an inward impression or outward sign. In either case, Moses would have to be attentive to God's direction. He could beat the wrong rock for days to no avail. What a helpful reminder to Moses that a servant is nothing without the Master.

The water was to come from a rock at the foot of Mount Sinai. This served a practical purpose but was also part of God's curriculum. The Israelites would camp at this location for the entire year to come. God had provided an abundant supply of water for their use during this time. God also taught them a lesson about himself. At Mount Sinai, they would learn what it meant to be the people of God, a God who was to them the very water of life.

God provided food and water for his people and an opportunity to rest. Exodus 16:23 marks the first time in the Bible the Israelites (or anyone) were commanded to rest on the Sabbath. They did not need to gather the manna on that day because God had provided enough on the preceding day. The Sabbath was a gift exchange. God gave them this day so they could rest from their labors. He also gave them the food they would need for that day and preserved it from spoiling as it ordinarily would have. In return, the Israelites were to give the day back to God; it was to be "a holy sabbath to the LORD" (v. 23). They were to honor him by not working, that is, by trusting him to provide. He gave them rest and provision; they gave him honor. This, in a nutshell, is the timeless exchange between God and humanity. We have been made for a relationship with him. He makes rest possible to those who will honor him by their faith-filled obedience. For the Israelites in the wilderness, God provided both physical rest and the opportunity for their souls to be at rest in him.

God provided something else to his people at that moment: protection (17:8–16). The Amalekites were a nomadic people, descended from Esau, who lived in the region of Rephidim. They could not have been pleased by the incursion of the Israelites into land they considered their own. Ancient animosity may have played a part in the conflict as well, but the Amalekites were probably more concerned about the Israelites as interlopers, given that food and water were scarce. And the Israelites were not empty-handed. They had plundered the Egyptians as they left; now the Amalekites appeared intent on plundering the Israelites.

Moses instructed his lieutenant, Joshua, mentioned here for the first time in the Bible, to prepare the Israelites for battle (v. 9). This would appear to be Joshua's first taste of warfare, providing him with experience that would be useful later. Moses also recruited Aaron, his brother, and Hur, a leader of the tribe of Judah. Their jobs were to assist Moses as he interceded in prayer for the Israelite warriors. Note the divine-human synergy: some hands bearing the sword and others lifted in prayer for God's intervention. In this way, God brought victory, protecting his people from their enemies.

In addition to material provision, physical and spiritual rest, and protection, God provided justice (18:1–27). Up to this point, Moses had taken full responsibility for ensuring justice for the Israelites. People would go to him with complaints about how they had been mistreated by another Israelite, and Moses would serve as a judge and render a decision. He probably assumed that this was part of his role as God's servant, however inefficient and taxing it proved to be to all concerned.

Into this well-intentioned but dysfunctional system stepped a foreigner. Although some foreigners and distant family members were out to harm Israel, others helped, like this Midianite. The Midianites were distant relatives through one of Abraham's other sons (see Gen. 25:2). Moses' father-in-law, Jethro, saw what was happening and suggested a better way to resolve disputes. Why not enlist "capable men" (Ex. 18:21), those who were reverent, trustworthy, and honest and delegate the responsibility to them? Moses would continue to instruct the people in God's law and hear the most difficult cases, but justice would be better served by sharing the load with others.

THE SERVANT IN THE WILDERNESS

Reflecting on what and how God provided for his people gives important insights into God's character and the lessons he taught his servants. God is able to provide using perfectly natural means. He does not appear to have invented the manna just for the Israelites. He most certainly did not invent quail just for this occasion. The springs of Elim were flowing long before the Israelites arrived. Though the timing and scope of the provision were miraculous, the food itself appears to have been naturally occurring commodities.

Although God often provides through natural means, he is also capable of providing in unusual ways. Take Jethro, for example. It is not uncommon for fathers-in-law to give advice, but to have God provide insight through a foreigner is most unusual. So are tossing trees into pools and hitting rocks as means to provide drinkable water. Who ever heard of winning a battle by holding up one's arms? And what about providing double manna one day and none the next? God's servants need to understand that our Master sometimes provides in surprising ways that boost our faith and in normal ways that are recognized as miraculous only through the eyes of faith.

And when God provides, his timing and portions are perfect. While his provision is free, it comes with stipulations, such as the instruction on when to gather manna. And God's provision comes in varied ways. Three times in these chapters God provided water to the Israelites, each time in a different way. As far as we know, the battle plan used to defeat the Amalekites was never employed again. Some describe God as a watchmaker who wound up the world only to let it run on its own, but that is not the God seen here. God is actively engaged with his people.

MORE THAN A MEAL

During the Sinai expedition, God was like a parent, providing for his children. He was also like a teacher on a field trip with students, eager to take advantage of every teachable moment. The main subject in God's lesson plan was faith. He wanted his people to learn what it meant to trust him. That is why he sent a supply of manna only for one day at a time. To earn their daily trust, he provided daily bread. This is why it was important that the Israelites name the places on their route, so they could recall the lessons. They could say to themselves, "Remember how God sweetened the waters at Bitter [that is Marah]?" (Ex. 15:23) or "Do you recall how we put God to the challenge at Testing [that is Massah] and quarreled at Quarreling [that is Meribah]?" (17:7). And they could recall, "See that altar over there, the one called 'Yahweh is My Banner?' There God used Moses' prayers with arms extended like a banner to bring us victory." To ensure that the Israelites would remember the lessons of the wilderness is also the reason God instructed them to place a jar of manna in the ark of the covenant (16:32–34). Even though they could not see the manna, they knew it remained there, free from maggots, as a testimony of God's faithful provision.

God gave reminders of each lesson in the wilderness, and he did something more. He gave exams. Any teacher will tell you that exams are not primarily to inform the teacher of the students' progress but to show the students where they stand. The teacher already has a pretty good idea of how well the students are doing. The test is a way to reinforce what has been learned and demonstrate areas of weakness. Twice in these chapters God is said to test his people (15:22–27; 16:4). On the first occasion, he allowed them to experience thirst to see how they would respond. The test was not for his benefit; he already knew how they would respond. The test was for their benefit, to give them an opportunity to demonstrate that they had learned an important lesson. The second test was whether they would follow God's instructions on gathering manna. God knew most would, but some would not. After the test, each person knew precisely where he or she stood in regard to obedience.

God wanted his servants to trust that he was present and he would provide. He wanted them to understand that the former guaranteed the latter. His specific instructions regarding the water from the rock were meant to reinforce this lesson. God also wanted the people to know that it was his assistance, not their military might, that brought victory. That is why their success in battle rose and fell with Moses' arms.

God wanted trust, and he knew that the people's faith would be dead if not accompanied by obedience. God could have sweetened the waters without the tree, but it was important for Moses to obey. God could have provided food in a variety of ways, but he made the provision conditional on following his directions. Others could help Moses carry the load of administering justice, but they had to be godly people.

God's insistence on Israelite obedience provides a clue to another item in God's lesson plan. He wanted to involve his people in his work. We have already seen God's insistence on partnering with people for doing what he could surely do on his own. When God provided, it was almost always in ways that required human cooperation, such as Moses tossing the tree or striking the rock, the daily gathering of manna, and the deputized judges. God's provision bears human fingerprints.

Trust without obedience is useless, and so is obedience unless done for God's glory and not our own. To trust and obey only in order to have enough to eat, experience physical rest, be safe, and receive justice is to use God like a vending machine. When you insert the proper amount of money, you always get what you bargained for. God refuses to be treated in such a manner. He is the sovereign ruler of the universe and insists that we honor him whether we get anything in return or not.

If we made a statement like that about a human being, we would have to conclude that the person had an ego the size of Texas. Yet we don't level this same criticism at God. Why not? Because God deserves our honor, not for what he does for us but simply for who he is. And because honoring God is always best for us. Think of it: God has existed for eternity; by comparison, humans have been around for the blink of an eye. Before our entrance, God was honored and glorified by the angels. If all God wanted was more glory, he would have created more angels. He created human beings in order to have a relationship with us, a relationship that reaches its fullest expression when we delight in him. This relationship is something like a marriage. Anyone blessed with a happy marriage will understand that marriage is most delightful when a husband honors his wife and vice versa. We exist to honor God, and we find that doing so results in our greatest joy. Thomas Aquinas, after reminding us that all human effort is directed to some end, noted that "no end of human works is so great as the honor of God."[6]

Immediately after God delivered the Israelites through the sea, they knew very well who was responsible for that deliverance:

Your right hand, LORD, *was majestic in power. Your right hand*, LORD, *shattered the enemy. In the greatness of your majesty you threw down those who opposed you. You unleashed your burning anger*; it consumed them like stubble. *By the blast of your nostrils* the waters piled up. The surging waters stood up like a wall; the deep waters congealed in the heart of the sea.

The enemy boasted, "I will pursue, I will overtake them. I will divide the spoils; I will gorge myself on them. I will draw my sword and my hand will destroy them." But *you blew with your breath*, and the sea covered them. They sank like lead in the mighty waters. *Who among the gods is like you, LORD? Who is like you—majestic in holiness, awesome in glory, working wonders? You stretch out your right hand*, and the earth swallows your enemies. *In your unfailing love you will lead the people you have redeemed. In your strength you will guide them to your holy dwelling.* (Ex. 15:6–13, emphasis added)

Not far into their journey, however, the Israelites blamed Moses for bringing them "out into this desert to starve" (16:3). Moses reminded them it was not he but God who had delivered them. They needed to honor him. God affirmed Moses' words by showing up in a dramatic fashion, with "the glory of the LORD appearing in the cloud" (v. 10). Israel needed to recognize and acknowledge God's glory.

God made this point also through Jethro's confession of faith. After hearing from his son-in-law all that Yahweh had done, Jethro testified, "Praise be to the LORD, who rescued you from the hand of the Egyptians and of Pharaoh, and who rescued the people from the hand of the Egyptians. Now I know that the LORD is greater than all other gods, for he did this to those who had treated Israel arrogantly" (18:10–11).

Honoring God is not something done once for all time. God's people must continually recognize and acknowledge his greatness. In a later moment of crisis, Moses chose to honor himself rather than God, and it cost him dearly (Num. 20). The Israelites had moved on from Mount Sinai and were traveling through the wilderness when they once again found themselves without water. God instructed Moses on what to do: accompanied by Aaron, he was to take his staff and speak to the rock (Num. 20:8). One gets the sense that God was testing Moses. Why else tell him to take along a staff he would not use? Would Moses take the easy way and revert back to an earlier moment of success, or would he trust God to do something new. A disturbing tone crept into Moses' voice on this occasion. He sounded more like a frustrated leader than a faithful servant: "Listen, you rebels, must we bring you water out of this rock?" (v. 10). Moses lifted his staff and struck the rock twice. Water gushed out, but so did God's judgment: Moses would not be the one to lead the Israelites into Canaan.

The punishment may seem too harsh for the crime, but the harshness merely shows how important it is that God receive the honor. Rather than trust God to provide water in a new way, Moses relied on his own judgment. He did things his way instead of God's way. Rather than being content as an instrument in God's hand, like the staff in his own hand, Moses tried to take center stage. Instead of allowing God to receive all the glory, Moses turned this into an opportunity to get a little credit for all he and Aaron had done. Israel needed water, and they got it. They also needed another opportunity to see the greatness of their God, but Moses turned the spotlight on himself instead.

We honor God by giving him the credit for what he has done. We need not minimize or dismiss our part in the divine-human partnership, but we must acknowledge to ourselves and to others that everything good comes from God. Even our ability to participate in God's work is the result of his grace. In a better moment, Moses—fully realizing God had used him in powerful ways—insisted to the Israelites that "it was the LORD who brought [them] out of Egypt" (Ex. 16:6).

A second way we honor God is by accepting his word, his promises, as true and obeying it. Moses believed God would turn the water sweet when he threw the tree into it; he did not express surprise at these instructions, he just obeyed. Honoring God by accepting and obeying his word applies to situations where he tells us exactly what our action or response should be; for example, gather manna every day except the Sabbath, strike that rock, turn the other cheek, forgive the one who maligned you, or do not defraud another person. We honor God when we do what he has told us to do.

This type of honor also is required when the Bible provides insight into larger life issues, such as what constitutes true greatness. We honor God when we first agree that true greatness is found not in power, wealth, or influence but in self-sacrificing service to others, and then demonstrate that agreement by behaving in that way. God is "the ruler of all things" (1 Chron. 29:12) so we know that all events are subject to his control. We honor God when we live in the hope that, despite how things may appear, God will sovereignly accomplish his eternal purpose.

CONCLUSION

In addition to the material things God provided for his people on their way to Mount Sinai, God provided important lessons on what it means to be his servants. Moses and the Israelites saw that God knew their needs and could meet those needs in both natural and unusual ways. They also saw that God was concerned about something beyond their physical needs. He also sought to form them into a people who faithfully obeyed his instructions and who were quick to give him the glory he deserved. These lessons were important preparation for what God was about to reveal to them at Sinai.

8

The Faithful Servant and the Liberating Law, Part 1

EXODUS 19–40

The events recorded in Exodus 19–40 took place while the Israelites were camped at Mount Sinai. Admittedly, these chapters are not as exciting as the action-packed first half of the book. However, what happened during this period is equally important. Without this, the earlier events would not likely have amounted to much. By receiving the law, Israel got to know their covenant God and understood what it means to serve such a Master. Through the law, God furthered the Israelites' transformation from a group of former slaves into a true nation. The law also provided wonderful insights into God's heart, revealing more about his character and redemptive plan.

GROUND RULES

Before giving the law, God set parameters for his people. Without a few clear ground rules, Moses and the Israelites would not fully comprehend what was about to happen to and for them or the great grace being shown them. These ground rules appear in Exodus 19, which describes Israel's arrival at Sinai and Moses' first encounter with God on the mountain.

God began by describing the basis for the covenant he had with Israel. It was he who had punished their oppressor, Egypt, and who had miraculously brought them to himself at Sinai. They had not liberated themselves but had been set free by God. They now were given the opportunity to be his "treasured possession" (Ex. 19:5). This phrase expresses a single Hebrew word, used here for the first time in the Old Testament. Other than the times it describes God's special interest in Israel (see Deut. 7:6; 14:2; 26:18; Ps. 135:4; Mal. 3:17), it is used to describe the wealth of a king (see 1 Chron. 29:3; Eccl. 2:8). Imagine how this must have sounded to the ears of those who until recently had been slaves in a foreign land.

Although the entire earth belonged to God, he had chosen this people. To go from being slaves to God's treasure would be remarkable enough, but God had more in mind for Israel. His plan was to make them into a kingdom of priests and a holy nation (Ex. 19:6). He wanted to set them apart from all other nations. They were to function in a priestly role on behalf of the rest of the world, representing God to the world and the world to God.

Many years earlier, God had promised the Israelites' forefather, Abraham, that his descendants would be a source of blessing to all nations (Gen. 12:3). No further explanation was given to Abraham as to how this would come about. One sees glimpses of this throughout Genesis, such as God's blessing of the non-Israelite Laban through Jacob, and God's blessing of Egypt through Joseph. However, the specific way in which Abraham's descendants would bless the world remained a mystery until Sinai. There God revealed that Israel would function as priest to the world, an intermediary between the nations and God.

THE FAITHFUL SERVANT AND THE LIBERATING LAW, PART 1

In the ancient world, priests were the human representatives of the god or gods whom they served. Priests ensured that the people understood the deity's expectations, assisted the people in meeting those expectations, and assured the people of the god's favor when they did so. As we will see in the next chapter, God would soon ordain a priesthood through Aaron's line, which would fulfill the priestly role for Israel. Israel, in turn, would take up this role on behalf of the rest of the world. The specifics of how they were to function in that role would be revealed over time.

Most of the law given in the succeeding chapters of Exodus focused primarily on the second part of God's plan for Israel: what it meant to be a holy nation. Their holiness began with God's holiness. To us, few things are more distasteful than someone who is self-righteous, and few things are more compelling than a person whose holiness has been absorbed by contact with the divine. God intended the latter for his people. He would take up residence with them as their invisible king. They would not need to make themselves holy. God would do that by fiat and formation, by pronouncement and by process.

Their holiness began with a demonstration of God's holiness. This is one reason for the smoke and fire, barriers restricting access, and the demands for consecration that occupy so much of Exodus 19. Before Israel could understand what it meant to become a holy people, they had to understand that they served a holy God. To do so, they had to experience a holy terror. This is what the Old Testament describes as the fear of the Lord. This experience is where wisdom begins (Prov. 9:10), where suffering finds solace (Job 28:28), and where life finds meaning (Eccl. 12:13). What the Old Testament describes as the fear of the Lord, the New Testament refers to as faith. To please God without faith is impossible (Heb. 11:6), so one cannot follow God without fearing him: "And now,

Israel, what does the LORD your God ask of you but to fear the LORD your God, to walk in obedience to him, to love him, to serve the LORD your God with all your heart and with all your soul, and to observe the LORD's commands and decrees that I am giving you today for your own good?" (Deut. 10:12–13).

It is ironic that though we usually flee from what we are afraid of, God commanded Israel to follow the one they feared. Moses addressed and maintained this tension when he commanded Israel, "Do not be afraid. God has come to test you, so that the fear of God will be with you to keep you from sinning" (Ex. 20:20). The truth is, only those who fear God *can* follow him, for by fearing him they eliminate all other fears.

A second reason for the dramatic manifestations of God's holiness was to validate Moses' role as leader of Israel (19:9). Much has changed since that day in terms of leadership. Our democratic and highly participatory culture weighs against the authoritarian leadership sanctioned by God in Exodus and exercised by Moses. I am convinced this transition to a more egalitarian form of leadership is as God intended and that he is pleased with humanity's effort to value the life and voice of each human being. What has not changed, however, is that God's people need leaders who have been with God and whose words and actions bear witness to that association. Moses had to understand that his authority rested not on himself but on his relationship with God. The faithful servant has no authority except what has been delegated to him by his Master.

THE FAITHFUL SERVANT AND THE LIBERATING LAW, PART 1

THE PURPOSE OF THE LAW

The law given to Moses, as recorded in the remainder of Exodus and all of Leviticus, was the means whereby God would develop holiness within Israel. Through the law, the Israelites would come to understand how holy people live and would immerse themselves in the process of becoming holy. It is a misconception that the law of Moses was given in order to bring Israel into a relationship with God. The Israelites already had a relationship with God, or else he would not have bothered to deliver them from Egypt and bring them to Sinai. The law of Moses was to the Israelites as the Sermon on the Mount is to Christians: not the means of salvation but a description of what salvation looks like in the life of a people.

Because the law was the means by which God fashioned Israel as a holy nation, unique in the world, some might imagine that the law itself was unique in the world. It was not. There are many similarities between the law of Moses and other law codes from the ancient Near East. For example, both the law of Moses and the earlier Code of Hammurabi contain laws dealing with stolen livestock, prescribing similar consequences for an offender.[1]

This should not trouble us because the authority of the Mosaic law does not rest on its uniqueness. The authority of the law rests on its author, namely God. The similarities between the law of Moses and that of Hammurabi or any other code exist because each expresses ways to carry out the moral law written by God on every human heart. Hammurabi and other lawgivers transmitted their laws as best they could, given the constraints of a conscience and reason infected by sin; that is, within the limitations of general revelation. Moses received his law through special revelation. While culturally conditioned, that is, based in the primitive, traditional, agricultural economy of the ancient Near East, the Mosaic law represents a much clearer picture of God's intent because it was communicated directly by God, without the distortions of sin in its transmission.

That the Mosaic law is an inspired yet culturally conditioned version of the moral law explains the way it is regarded by the apostle Paul in the book of Romans. In some passages that Mosaic law is described as arousing "sinful passions" (7:5), as "brought in so that the trespass might increase" (5:20), and as bringing death (7:11). Yet Paul, in the same letter, described the law as "holy, righteous and good" (7:12). Christians have died to the law (7:6), yet we must still obey it (8:1–4).

How can both be true? Because the Mosaic law represents a culturally conditioned and limited expression of the inescapable, eternally binding moral law that is written on the heart of every person. Christians today are no longer obligated to obey the law of Moses because we are not its original recipients, but we are obligated to keep the moral law. In some passages in the law of Moses, the moral law appears clearly. Most would agree that the Ten Commandments are a clear expression of the moral law. At such points, we follow the moral law as it meets the Mosaic law.

The heart of both the Mosaic law and the moral law is the Ten Commandments (Ex. 20:1–17). Jews and Christians agree that there are ten of these commandments but have numbered them in three different ways. For Jews, the first statement is a commandment and not a word of introduction: "I am the LORD your God, who brought you out of Egypt, out of the land of slavery" (v. 2). The second commandment combines the prohibitions against other gods and making idols. The succeeding commandments address: (3) not misusing God's name, (4) remembering the Sabbath, (5) honoring parents, (6) not murdering, (7) not committing adultery, (8) not stealing, (9) not giving false testimony, and (10) not coveting.

THE FAITHFUL SERVANT AND THE LIBERATING LAW, PART 1

Roman Catholics and Lutherans count ten commands by starting with the combined prohibitions against having other gods and making idols as the first commandment, but ending with two commandments concerning covetousness: (9) not coveting your neighbor's house, and (10) not coveting your neighbor's wife or property. For Orthodox Christians, as well as Reformed and most other Protestants, there is a third way of reaching ten:

1. Have no other gods before God.
2. Do not make or worship idols.
3. Do not misuse God's name.
4. Remember the Sabbath day.
5. Honor your parents.
6. Do not murder.
7. Do not commit adultery.
8. Do not steal.
9. Do not give false testimony.
10. Do not covet.

While it is appropriate to refer to these ten as legally binding commandments or laws, they contain no mention of penalty should they be broken. For this reason, it may be better to understand these as ten descriptions for how God's covenant people should live. There is no mention of what would happen to them if people broke one of these since breaking them would have been unthinkable for the faithful Israelites. The Ten Commandments compare more closely with the obligations of citizenship than with laws. The United States Department of Homeland Security identifies these responsibilities of a US citizen:

- Support and defend the Constitution.
- Stay informed of the issues affecting your community.
- Participate in the democratic process.
- Respect and obey federal, state, and local laws.
- Respect the rights, beliefs, and opinions of others.
- Participate in your local community.
- Pay income and other taxes honestly, and on time, to federal, state, and local authorities.
- Serve on a jury when called upon.
- Defend the country if the need should arise.[2]

Obviously, these duties imply obedience to many laws, but the responsibilities themselves rise above specifics to define more general obligations. The purpose of the law as expressed in the Ten Commandments is similar: to define the fundamental obligations of those who are citizens in God's covenant community.

The first half of these commandments describes how one loves God, the second half describes how to love one's neighbor. Loving God requires wholehearted loyalty, no other gods introduced as rivals, not even physical images of Yahweh that could potentially detract from the relationship he desires. Loving God includes the expectation that his people will honor his name, neither taking it lightly nor employing it in deceptive, manipulative, or superstitious ways. They will also acknowledge his lordship on a weekly basis by giving up a day of labor to observe a Sabbath rest. Those who love God also welcome the chain of authority he has put in place, beginning as it does with one's own parents.

Loving one's neighbor implies valuing the life of the neighbor, as well as that neighbor's marriage and personal possessions. Love for neighbor is expressed through a love for justice. The prohibition against "false witness" is not so much a ban on lying as on failing to

THE FAITHFUL SERVANT AND THE LIBERATING LAW, PART 1

accurately represent the truth in court, thereby contributing to the perversion of justice.

The final commandment is not an afterthought but represents the core of the rest, namely, one's attitude. The primary focus of covetousness is one's attitude toward possessions, but it can manifest itself in other ways. The opposite of covetousness is not mere contentment but complete loyalty and submission to God, loving him with one's whole heart, and loving one's neighbor as oneself.

The purpose of the Mosaic law was to provide an inspired yet culturally specific version of the moral law so God's people would know how to love him and each other. Love for God and others summarizes how God's holy people were meant to live. Yet how could the Israelites maintain their holiness, loving God and others as they should? And what would love look like when it came to specifics? Anticipating these questions, God blessed Israel with the necessary details.

The rabbis who counted the laws given through Moses concluded that there are 613. These included laws about what kind of cloth to use in making clothing, how to maintain ritual purity, when and how to worship, what to do in case of a skin disease, what to do with the produce one grew, which kinds of animals were permissible as food, how to pass along an inheritance, and how to cook certain foods, for example.

This specificity in the law of Moses has fostered a misunderstanding about the character of God, namely that he is intent on meddling in people's private lives, spoiling their fun, and draining precious resources for his own glory. Nothing could be further from the truth. God's demands are surprisingly limited given all he had done for Israel. The specificity of the law was his gift to the people. As any parent will tell you, general principles do not work well in guiding children; they need specific instructions. Israel was new to following God, and his instructions were meant to lighten, not add to, their burden. When God spoke to the Israelites about the law, he described it as within reach:

> Now what I am commanding you today is not too difficult for you or beyond your reach. It is not up in heaven, so that you have to ask, "Who will ascend into heaven to get it and proclaim it to us so we may obey it?" Nor is it beyond the sea, so that you have to ask, "Who will cross the sea to get it and proclaim it to us so we may obey it?" No, the word is very near you; it is in your mouth and in your heart so you may obey it. (Deut. 30:11–14)

God's supposed meddling in personal life was actually helpful to the Israelites in helping them understand that holiness resides not only in public places of worship but in private places as well, in the ordinary stuff of life. Circumcision provided a wonderful illustration of this point. And in this way, God gave his people a wonderful gift. While other nations practiced circumcision, none performed the operation on infant boys or in the same way. Even more important than the health and sanitation benefits of circumcision, it provided a frequent reminder that the Israelites were a marked people, unique in the world, chosen by God to be a kingdom of priests and a holy nation.

Judging by what Old Testament believers said about the law, they certainly did not see it as burdensome or invasive. They celebrated it as evidence of God's concern for them. Other gods in the ancient world did not fully commit themselves to their people, withholding important information so their devotees were left in the dark. Israelites knew precisely what Yahweh expected of them, for he had revealed his will clearly and in detail through the law of Moses. So they sang its praises; in fact, the longest psalm in the psalter, Psalm 119, spends the entirety of its 176 verses singing about the blessings of the Mosaic law. The Israelites understood that these 613 laws were God's way of helping them be a holy people.

God declared Israel a holy nation (Ex. 19:6), and he wanted them to live like it. So he gave them the Mosaic law to help them do so. Holiness is essentially separation for a sacred purpose; God wanted the Israelites to be separate from the surrounding nations so they could accomplish God's purpose of blessing those nations.

We tend to react against those who choose to separate themselves in order to be more holy. We criticize such people for withdrawing from the world in which God calls us to be salt and light. Though such criticisms do have some merit, they fail to recognize that separation may be necessary in certain circumstances. We recognize that fist bumps rather than handshakes may be more appropriate during flu season. Who blames young parents for keeping their infant home from the nursery when illness is rampant? The Israelites were in their spiritual infancy at the exodus, and the world into which they had come was rife with moral corruption. Because they had the important mission to bless all nations, the spiritual health of the Israelites was especially important.

Many of the laws were intended to keep the Israelites spiritually healthy by maintaining their distinctiveness as a people. They were forbidden to intermarry with their neighbors because kinship would make it easier to slip into idolatry (see Deut. 7:3). Some laws limited social interaction between Israel and its neighbors, other laws prohibited certain mourning rituals practiced by the Canaanites (see Lev. 19:27–28). Israelites were prohibited from eating certain types of meat and all meat that was not properly prepared. Many social gatherings (such as weddings, funerals, weaning of children, visits, farewells) involved food, so having a restricted diet made participation in such gatherings with foreigners less likely.

God's promise to bless all nations through Israel, first delivered to Abraham, would become clear over time. The New Testament apostles finally recognized it as a prediction of the gospel message. That was how Peter explained it to Jews in Jerusalem: "And you are heirs of the prophets and of the covenant God made with your fathers. He said to Abraham, 'Through your offspring all peoples on earth will be blessed'" (Acts 3:25). Paul was even more specific in writing to the Galatians: "Understand, then, that those who have faith are children of Abraham. Scripture foresaw that God would justify the Gentiles by faith, and announced the gospel in advance to Abraham: 'All nations will be blessed through you.' So those who rely on faith are blessed along with Abraham, the man of faith" (Gal. 3:7–9).

Given that the law was crucial to helping Israel accomplish this goal, it is not surprising to discover many insights into the gospel in the law. As noted earlier, the gospel meant reconciliation between humans and God, interpersonal and intrapersonal reconciliation, and reconciliation between humanity and the natural world. God provided the Mosaic law, in part, to help his people understand how these relationships would one day be healed.

Many of the laws concern the first and most important relationship, between humans and God. Restoration of all four relationships is beautifully anticipated in a vision held out for those who keep the law:

> If you follow my decrees and are careful to obey my commands, I will send you rain in its season, and the ground will yield its crops and the trees their fruit. Your threshing will continue until grape harvest and the grape harvest will continue until planting, and you will eat all the food you want and live in safety in your land.

THE FAITHFUL SERVANT AND THE LIBERATING LAW, PART 1

I will grant peace in the land, and you will lie down and no one will make you afraid. I will remove wild beasts from the land, and the sword will not pass through your country. You will pursue your enemies, and they will fall by the sword before you. Five of you will chase a hundred, and a hundred of you will chase ten thousand, and your enemies will fall by the sword before you.

I will look on you with favor and make you fruitful and increase your numbers, and I will keep my covenant with you. You will still be eating last year's harvest when you will have to move it out to make room for the new. I will put my dwelling place among you, and I will not abhor you. I will walk among you and be your God, and you will be my people. I am the LORD your God, who brought you out of Egypt so that you would no longer be slaves to the Egyptians; I broke the bars of your yoke and enabled you to walk with heads held high. (Lev. 26:3–13; see also Deut. 28:1–13)

God gave the law to his people both so they would be holy, loving him and each other wholeheartedly, and so they would be a source of blessing for all peoples. Also, God gave the law as a roadmap to help them navigate in a fallen world. God had planned for the ultimate solution to the problem of sin, and he cared enough about his people to provide a temporary solution, one that would make life easier for them until the ultimate solution was set in place.

Today we would call such a temporary solution a work-around. A missionary friend of mine told of a time when his vehicle broke down in a remote part of the African country where he served. The fan belt had broken, and he was far from the nearest auto parts store. As he tells the story, an African man rode up on a bicycle. Combining two of the many wonderful African qualities—generosity and ingenuity—this stranger created a temporary fan belt out of the inner tube from his bike, enabling my friend to drive to a place where he could buy the proper part.

God provided something like this for the Israelites through the law of Moses—work-arounds showing how to live in a fallen world until the ultimate solution could be provided. The tabernacle, priesthood, sacrificial system, and festival calendar were both tools, to teach Israel how to understand the ultimate solution when it arrived, and work-arounds, temporary solutions to the problem of sin. God knew that his people needed to have a relationship with him, but he knew also that the relationship could not reach its optimal status before Christ came. In the meantime, he provided temporary ways for the Israelites to experience fellowship with God.

The Mosaic law also provided temporary solutions for the problem of interpersonal and intrapersonal alienation. The law places a high value on marriage and celebrates marital union. Although marriage was instituted prior to the fall of humanity, post-fall it serves as one of God's best work-arounds. God provided numerous opportunities for celebration in the law, additional ways to foster healthy relationships between people and within each person. Many of the commandments ease sin's impact on nature. Because of the curse, working seven days without rest brings exhaustion, so God commanded the Israelites to observe the Sabbath. Planting the same crops year after year depletes a field's nutrients, so God commanded them to give their fields a rest from planting every seventh year. Even with such protections, people are bound to fall on hard times, so God instituted laws to help them get back on their feet economically. The Jubilee is one example, which resets the economy every fifty years. In these and other ways, God assisted his people as they lived within a fallen world, until such time as his ultimate solution would be put into effect.

THE FAITHFUL SERVANT AND THE LIBERATING LAW, PART 1

The Mosaic law served at least one other purpose. Through these commandments, God liberated his people. The first half of Exodus describes how God got Israel out of Egypt; the second half tells how God would get Egypt out of Israel. For more than four centuries, Israel had lived first as foreigners in and finally as slaves to a foreign nation. It would take more than a change of address to change their self-identity. Concepts like the dignity of human life, the purpose of marriage, the importance of private property, and the significance of justice meant one thing to slaves but something very different to free people, particularly those whose freedom was intended to bring true freedom for all people. For centuries the Israelites had been steeped in polytheism and misunderstanding of the jealous nature of the true God. God used the law of Moses to liberate them from their inaccurate and inadequate understanding of themselves and himself.

The Mosaic law shaped the Israelites into the people God wanted them to be. It also shaped those who would serve the Israelites as leaders, especially Moses. As God began to reveal his law, he made a point of elevating Moses in the eyes of the people. This was an important step in building Moses' self-confidence. His role markedly changed at Mount Sinai as he transitioned from the leader of an expedition to the one who led the people both materially and spiritually. He learned a lesson at Mount Sinai that he would put into practice often: He must stand between the people and a holy, jealous God; he must explain God's will to them and intercede for them when they deviate from it.

God did not elevate Moses for his benefit alone but for the benefit of the people. They needed to know Moses had God's ear and they had a way to hear from God. Our egalitarian culture reacts against the idea that some people have special access to God. While there are certainly benefits to our contemporary view, democratizing religion can be taken too far so that everyone is his or her own Moses.

The ideal would be to balance the ideas that God's Spirit is given to all believers and that he continues to call certain individuals to places of spiritual authority (as well as holding them to a higher degree of responsibility).

CONCLUSION

The first half of the book of Exodus describes the rescue of God's people from Egypt; the second half describes their liberation from the mind-set of slavery and transformation into the people of God. The law of Moses was a crucial part of this latter freedom, clarifying the truth about Israel and its God. In the next chapter, we continue our exploration of this law, focusing on Israel's worship. God had more lessons to teach Moses and the Israelites about what it meant to serve him faithfully.

9

The Faithful Servant and the Liberating Law, Part 2

Exodus 19–40

While the Israelites remained at Mount Sinai, God continued to instruct Moses and his people, both from the Ten Commandments and through regulations regarding the place and manner of proper worship. Three insights stand out prominently in this part of God's curriculum: his willingness to accommodate himself to a human level of understanding, his nature as a gracious provider, and his high expectations of his people.

THE GOD WHO STOOPS

God had been gracious to the Israelites, rescuing them from Egyptian bondage and giving them a liberating law. God's grace was even more apparent when, in Exodus 25:8, he commanded them to construct a sanctuary for him, saying, "I will dwell among them." Yahweh would travel with his people; what a remarkable thought! This God, whom they had only recently come to know, would reside in their midst. A cloud that glowed with fire at night marked his presence over the tabernacle. There, visible to all Israelites day or night, was tangible evidence that Yahweh was in their midst (40:38). They needed only to lift their eyes to gain reassurance that God was with them.

God's tent was situated in the middle of the camp, and each of the tribes placed in their designated spot around this center. While it was a great privilege to have Yahweh in their midst, it also brought great danger. Yahweh's holiness was like high voltage electricity: careless encounters could be fatal. So God instructed the Levites, those schooled in Yahweh's holiness, to camp between the tabernacle and the rest of the tribes.

The design of the camp, with Yahweh's tent in the middle and the people surrounding closely, resembled the design of an army on military encampment in the ancient Near East. We see examples from Egypt and in the Old Testament of the army camping around the king, who was at the center (see 1 Sam. 26:5). Israel was God's army, and the tabernacle was God's palace, the residence of the Divine King dwelling among them.

The Israelites were well acquainted with sanctuaries; Egypt was filled with them, majestic and massive stone monuments brimming with sacred imagery. However, the tabernacle was to be a very different kind of sanctuary from those temples of stone. It would be constructed of fabric and animal skins, set up with poles and bases. The few pieces of furniture would be light enough to carry on the shoulders of several men; they would be easily transportable, having attached rings through which poles could be inserted for carrying. The palace had to be portable because the Israelites were on a journey to Canaan. Yahweh was not only their king but also their guide. When the cloud that marked his divine presence "lifted from above

THE FAITHFUL SERVANT AND THE LIBERATING LAW, PART 2

the tabernacle [the Israelites] would set out; but if the cloud did not lift, they did not set out—until the day it lifted" (Ex. 40:36–37).

Taking up residence in a central, highly visible fashion was one way Yahweh stooped to accommodate the needs of his people. There was another, one more subtle but still crucial. Although some of the Israelite religion was unique, especially its absence of divine imagery, much of it was similar to the religions of its neighbors. The use of sacrifices, priests, and even the design of the tabernacle were similar to that of other peoples in the ancient Near East. Rather than require his people to completely relearn what it meant to worship, Yahweh adapted existing practices with which they were familiar. To avoid confusion between his worship and that required by other gods, Yahweh explained the true purposes for these practices.

For example, sacrifice was an essential part of ancient Near Eastern worship. In those other religions, however, sacrifices were a way to feed the deity. Yahweh instructed his people to offer sacrifices also, but not as his food. These sacrifices were to feed his servants, the priests. One type of sacrifice, the peace offering, was even used to feed the offerer and his invited guests at a celebratory meal. In other words, God employed the same practice, but reversed its purpose: rather than the worshipers feeding God, he fed them.

Religions in the ancient Near East had priests who represented the people to the deity and the deity to the people. God appointed priests for his people as well, beginning with Aaron and continuing through his descendants. In addition, Yahweh designated the whole nation as a "kingdom of priests" (19:6). What Aaron and his sons were to the nation of Israel, the nation was to the rest of the world.

Many temples in the ancient world were built in three sections, which moved the worshiper from holy to holier to holiest territory. God instructed his tabernacle to be built with this same design: from the courtyard with the bronze altar and laver; to the Holy Place with the table of bread, the lampstand, and the gold altar of incense to the Holy of Holies. In other sanctuaries, the inner sanctum contained a statue of the deity. In God's tabernacle, there was no statue, only a chest topped with cherubim representing his throne, where the invisible Yahweh sat. It was there, Yahweh promised Moses, "I will meet with you and give you all my commands for the Israelites" (25:22).

God certainly could have invented an entirely new way to worship him, one completely dissimilar to the worship practices of the ancient Near East. Such novelty would have been a fitting demonstration that there is one true God over the many crude representations worshiped by other nations. By inventing this entirely new religion, God would also have made it more difficult for his people to slip into syncretism, combining the worship of the true God with the views and practices of other religions.

However, imagine how difficult it would have been for Israel to practice this new religion. They would have had to unlearn everything they had known and replace it with brand new concepts and practices. It would have been like forcing a kindergarten Sunday school class to read the New Testament in Greek. God had the choice of either demanding that his people ascend closer to his level or stooping to theirs. He chose to stoop. Just as we oversimplify complex theological concepts so kindergartners can understand, God accommodated himself to what the Israelites could understand. He wanted a relationship with these people, so he met them where they were.

God always stoops to our level of understanding. He begins where we are. We see this throughout the Old Testament as God revealed himself in ways people could understand: as a warrior king, a mother hen, a bridegroom, a shepherd, a potter. And this is the key point of the New Testament: God stooped to be present with people in the person of Christ so the world would come to know him.

At Mount Sinai, God revealed his heart to his people. He made clear to what lengths he would go in order to have a relationship with them. He was their Master, and they were his servants, but they could count on him to meet them more than halfway. He would make the first move; he would stoop to serve them. As his servants, they would need to stoop as well. If the Master was willing to serve, certainly the servants should do the same. Servants do not exist for their own sakes but for others. God had not chosen Abraham and his descendants to be a reservoir of God's grace but the channel through which that grace would flow to bless the nations (see Gen. 12:3).

THE GOD WHO PROVIDES

The tabernacle system also revealed God's nature as generous provider. The Israelites had seen this in the wilderness as God had provided manna, quail, Sabbath rest, and more. God continued to provide for them through the tabernacle. We see this in the very first command God made regarding its construction. The Israelites were encouraged to bring an offering to Yahweh as they felt prompted in their hearts (Ex. 25:1–2). These offerings were to include the material needed to build the tabernacle: gold, silver, bronze, dyed yarn, linen, goat hair, animal skins, acacia wood, oil, spices, and precious stones. The Israelites had spent the past four centuries living in a foreign land, most recently as slaves. Where would they get such luxuries as these? God had provided Israel with these items, courtesy of the Egyptians. Remember, they were to go to their Egyptian neighbors just before their departure on Passover night to ask for items such as these. The very gifts they were invited to give to God, were items God had already given to them through the Egyptians.

God provided the materials to build the tabernacle and its furniture. He even provided the builders, enduing them with his divine Spirit. Yahweh told Moses:

> See, I have chosen Bezalel son of Uri, the son of Hur, of the tribe of Judah, and I have filled him with the Spirit of God, with wisdom, with understanding, with knowledge and with all kinds of skills—to make artistic designs for work in gold, silver and bronze, to cut and set stones, to work in wood, and to engage in all kinds of crafts. Moreover, I have appointed Oholiab son of Ahisamak, of the tribe of Dan, to help him. Also I have given ability to all the skilled workers to make everything I have commanded you. (31:2–6)

God provided for the construction of the tabernacle and for its ongoing ministry. The Israelites were to bring their animal, grain, and oil to sacrifice to God, but what they had to give, they had already been given. Yahweh made it clear that he did not need their sacrifices. "Every animal in the forest is [his], and the cattle on a thousand hills." What use would he have for "a bull from your stall or . . . goats from your pens"? God would say "if [he was] hungry . . . for the world is [his], and all that is in it" (Ps. 50:9–12). If Israel was obedient, God would continue to share his abundance with them. He would "open the heavens, the storehouse of his bounty, to send rain on [the] land in season and to bless all the work of [their] hands" (Deut. 28:12). He would give to them what they were in turn to give back to him.

God also provided the necessary instruction. In addition to gifting the workmen, God gave them the blueprint they were to follow in constructing the tabernacle (see Ex. 25:9). Much of the rest of Exodus and Leviticus explains the processes of building the tabernacle and

THE FAITHFUL SERVANT AND THE LIBERATING LAW, PART 2

worshiping Yahweh. Although some of this material is tedious to read, the ancient Israelite delighted in the detail, learning from every word.

Some aspects of the design and material of the tabernacle and its furniture was symbolic; it spoke volumes about God's character, Israel's nature and purpose, and God's redemptive plan. To unpack all these lessons would take us well beyond the scope of this book, but we can identify a few of the more obvious insights. This was a portable sanctuary because the Israelites and their King were on the move. They were headed to a land that Yahweh was going to give them, a land they had been promised centuries earlier. They were not nomads but pilgrims, and they worshiped a God who was willing to accompany them on the journey.

Although portable, the tabernacle was beautiful and opulent. Its brilliant colors—blue, white, purple, scarlet—shone in the sun as did the precious gems on the high priest's garments. The sights, sounds, and smells of the sacrifices mingling with the burning incense presented a magnificent and multisensory picture of a holy nation actively engaged with its God.

As worshipers passed through the opening of the tabernacle into the courtyard, they understood themselves to be entering sacred ground. The closer they moved to the bronze altar where offerings burned, the more they would have understood that Yahweh deserved their best. He could only be approached through sacrifice. Even the priests, those designated to represent the people to God, had to prepare themselves before entering Yahweh's palace. They had to wear the proper clothing, carry the proper items, and wash themselves in the bronze laver, or basin.

The priests alone could enter that palace. No person, however rich or pious, could have access to God except vicariously, through the priest. The rest of the people could only watch as their representative slipped through the curtain and into the Holy Place. They knew the priests would regularly replace the loaves on the table with fresh bread, symbolizing that Yahweh provides his people with food. They knew that when the priests placed the special incense on the golden altar, sweet-smelling smoke would ascend, representing the prayers of the Israelites going up to God. The Holy Place was illuminated by a golden lampstand holding small golden bowls of oil. The tiny flames from the burning wicks reflected off the gold of the lampstand, scattering light onto the interior of the Holy Place. This light represented the life God had given to his people—to each one individually, and to the nation as a whole.

Once a year in the fall, on the Day of Atonement (Yom Kippur), the high priest went through the Holy Place, through the second curtain into the Most Holy Place, to the ark of the covenant. There he would burn incense to create a veil of smoke and sprinkle the blood of a bull and a goat to atone for all the sins the Israelites had committed during the preceding year. The worshipers who stood in the courtyard knew they could never make that journey to the Most Holy Place. They also knew that God had provided someone to go in their stead, someone whose efforts on their behalf would gain God's favor.

All humans were created for interpersonal relationships, so God provided ways for his people to experience the blessing of a community of faith. Multiple times each year, people were invited to participate in sacred festivals. Some were simple, like the weekly Sabbath observance in which everyone rested from their labors. There was also the monthly observance of the new moon (see 1 Sam. 20), and a celebration at the fulfillment of a vow. In the latter instance, one could bring an animal to the sanctuary and slaughter it there. After the priest had taken his share (that is, his fee) and another small portion had been burnt on the bronze altar, the rest of the animal was returned to the worshiper. He or she would use that animal as the main course for a celebratory meal during which the host would recount how God had answered prayer. It was a combination potluck supper and testimony meeting.

Other opportunities were more elaborate, like the Feasts of Unleavened Bread, Pentecost, and Tabernacles. On these occasions, all Israelite men were to travel to the sanctuary where they would observe extensive celebrations involving offerings and other rituals. These were occasions of great joy as Yahweh's people celebrated the gracious provision of their God. The psalmist spoke of going to the temple "under the protection of the Mighty One with shouts of joy and praise among the festive throng" (Ps. 42:4). Even the pilgrimage to Jerusalem was a time of celebration. News that the time for the festival had come filled the psalmist with joy: "I rejoiced with those who said to me, 'Let us go to the house of the LORD'" (122:1).

Periodically, God's people would become ineligible to enter the sanctuary precincts. Sometimes that was due to their sinful action. At most times, however, ineligibility came through no fault of one's own, such as when a woman was having her period, a couple had engaged in sexual relations, someone had killed a wild animal for food, someone had buried a dead relative, or someone had contracted an infectious skin disease. This type of ineligibility is known in the Mosaic law as *uncleanness*. Because entering God's presence in the sanctuary is the right and responsibility of each Israelite, being unable to do so was a cause for concern.

Here again we find that God has made provision. Those who committed a sin could bring an animal for a burnt offering or sin offering, confess their sin, and watch their guilt go up in smoke. It was not the sacrifice that took away the sin; God did that by grace through faith. The sacrifice was their way of showing their deep repentance and obedience.

God also provided means by which an unclean person could become clean. Although these procedures—indeed, the very idea of unavoidable uncleanness—may seem strange to us, we should not miss the significance of the fact that God made a way for a person to become clean. Becoming clean involved the removal of the source of contamination, a period of time, and often a sacrifice, all under the supervision of a priest. Through this system, God taught his people an essential truth about himself: He is their King; they cannot come into his presence without preparation, without consecration, and without a gift in their hands. God provided both a lesson about his otherness and a way for his people to enter his presence. Do not miss the paradox: He is wholly other, but he welcomes his people who are properly prepared.

In these laws governing Israelite worship, we see God's gracious work-around to help his people live in a fallen world. Sin left them unable to experience unhindered fellowship with God, a problem he would ultimately solve in Christ. In the meantime, God implemented a way for the Israelites to experience some measure of fellowship. As often as they wished and so long as they were eligible, they could enter his courts with praise. God even provided priests and Levites to explain to his people how they could enjoy this fellowship more fully.

God provided in at least one other way through Israelite worship, though the worshipers themselves may not have fully comprehended it. Through the laws governing worship, God prepared his people for the Messiah so that when he arrived they would understand who he was and what he had come to do. When John the Baptist referred to Christ as "the Lamb of God, who takes away the sin of the world" (John 1:29), those who heard him understood what he was saying because they had been given the law. When the writer of Hebrews spoke of Christ as the eternal High Priest, his readers understood because they knew the law. The Mosaic law in general and the ceremonial portion in particular, provided the first Christians with helpful hooks on which to hang what they heard and saw concerning Jesus.

Yahweh's gracious provision would have made a deep impression on Moses and the Israelites, God's servants. They would have recognized that generosity is a fundamental value in God's household. We have all visited homes where stinginess was a core value—tiny portions, pained provision, giving with a grudge—homes we cannot escape from quickly enough. We have also known homes where generosity was the specialty of the house—the host was happy to give, no request was too much, plenty of food and laughter—homes we do not want to leave. This is what it is like to live in God's household. His servants must understand and embrace this. We serve a generous God whose mercies "are new every morning" (Lam. 3:23), who anoints our heads with oil, fills our cups to overflowing, and pursues us with "goodness and love . . . all the days" of our lives (Ps. 23:6).

THE GOD WHO MAKES DEMANDS

The Master was and is a gracious and generous God, but he held the Israelites accountable. The law of Moses contains sobering demands with serious consequences for those who neglect them. For example, Yahweh insists on being worshiped. The Israelites did not consider this unreasonable. In the ancient world, everyone understood the need to worship a god. Unlike many today, people in ancient times recognized that they were not at the pinnacle of the universe's pecking order. They knew they were not in complete control and that supernatural forces determined human destiny. To worship was to give the gods their due.

Yet Israel's God demanded something more. He insisted on being worshiped *exclusively*: "You shall have no other gods before me" (Ex. 20:3). Although many people recognized a chief deity, the ancients assumed that when it came to gods, the more the merrier. The more gods you worshiped, the greater your chances of success and happiness. This was polytheism, not the worship of a single god to the exclusion of all others.

The Israelites were not even allowed to fashion an image of God or the image of anything else to assist them in worship (vv. 4–6). They had spent the past four centuries in Egypt where divine images were everywhere and always accorded the greatest respect. Image-free worship must have seemed unusual, but God insisted on having the Israelites' exclusive reverence, no rivals allowed.

God made this point in the Ten Commandments, but the Israelites did not quite understand. This explains the fiasco of the golden calf (see Ex. 32). Moses had been on Mount Sinai a long time, and the people were not even sure he was still alive, what with all the fire, smoke, and earthquakes. Moses had been God's spokesman, so without him they had no way of knowing what to do next. They instructed Aaron to make a god to lead them.[1] When Aaron saw that his initial lack of courage had fostered idolatry, he tried to counter it by declaring a festival to Yahweh. But the Lord is a jealous God; worship of a false god can never be made right, even by pious devotion to the true God. The only thing to do with an idol is to destroy it so completely that it can never be restored. It must be shown for what it really is, a source of defilement. One of the terms used for "idols" might be rendered as "dung," a term which frequently appears in Ezekiel. Perhaps the prophet was alluding to the golden calf incident; what the Israelites had once worshiped was now only golden flecks in their waste.

THE FAITHFUL SERVANT AND THE LIBERATING LAW, PART 2

When it came to where and how the Israelites worshiped, God was also quite specific. He prescribed the design of the tabernacle and all its furnishings, passing on those patterns to Moses on the mountain (Ex. 25:9). As noted above, God was generous in providing the materials but was also demanding in how those materials were to be used. Though temporary, the beauty, design, and opulence of the tabernacle witnessed to the respect God deserved and demanded.

Yahweh insisted that all worship happen at the sanctuary. Apparently, the Israelites were accustomed to worshiping wherever they happened to be, even in an open field. God informed Moses that this must change. Sacrifices were to be offered only in the tabernacle (see Lev. 17:1–9). Later generations of Israelites would become careless at this point, worshiping Yahweh on hilltops and other high places. It took courageous King Hezekiah to put a stop to such activity and redirect all worship to the temple in Jerusalem, earning high praise from God for his righteous policy (see 2 Kings 18:1–5).

God designated the time for worship as well as the location. Three times each year, every Israelite man was required to make a pilgrimage to the sanctuary. When they arrived, they had to have a gift for their Divine King, who had graced them with his presence and blessed their fields. As God had said, "No one is to appear before me empty-handed" (Ex. 23:15; 34:20; see also Deut. 16:16). The gifts were to express their gratitude to Yahweh and to perform the rituals he required.

Worship at this central location had to be carried out precisely as Yahweh instructed. A gift had to be brought out of respect for the Divine King, who had honored them with his presence. Only those not disqualified by uncleanness could come. As Jesus later pointed out, even those graciously invited to the wedding feast must wear the proper clothing (see Matt. 22:11–14).

God was specific about what brought about disqualification. Any meat improperly bled was defiling. So was any animal without a split hoof and which did not chew its cud. Fish had to have both scales and fins. Certain birds were off-limits as were most types of insects. God did not say why some creatures were acceptable and not others, why birthing a daughter made a mother unclean for twice as long as if she birthed a boy, why a certain type of skin disease made someone unclean, or why defilement resulted from menstruation, a nosebleed, or touching a dead family member. However, God made it clear that he has the right to designate the difference and to demand obedience from his people.

The means of restoring purity after uncleanness were also carefully specified. Those means included removing the contaminant through burial, washing, or burning; waiting for a period of time; being restored to the community; and, often, performing some type of ritual. These means alone were not enough. The priest—God's representative—had to pronounce one clean.

Five major types of offerings were delineated in the law, which specified the kinds of animals that were acceptable, what the person making the offering was to do, what the priest was to do, and how to dispose of any remaining parts. In the case of the sin offering, the animal alone would not suffice for atonement. The penitent had to place his or her hands on the animal's head, symbolically identifying with the doomed animal.

Carelessness in carrying out the rituals could be deadly, as demonstrated by the fate of Aaron's sons, Nadab and Abihu (see Lev. 10:1–11; Num. 3:4; 26:61). Precisely what went wrong in their case is unclear. Perhaps they used their own equipment in making the sacrifice rather than the articles in the tabernacle. In that case "unauthorized fire" (Lev. 10:1) would refer to the pans in which the fire was carried. Perhaps they took the coals from the wrong place.

THE FAITHFUL SERVANT AND THE LIBERATING LAW, PART 2

Perhaps their equipment and technique were acceptable but the actions were done in the wrong order. They had just witnessed the potency of God's holiness as "fire came out from the presence of the LORD" (v. 1)—perhaps from the Most Holy Place, perhaps from heaven—and incinerated the sacrifice on the bronze altar. Carelessness on their part would have been inexcusable. Many scholars believe Nadab and Abihu were drunk. If so, they would have been less careful, and that would explain the warning given in verses 8–10 against priests drinking on duty. Whatever the reason for their death, God was clearly displeased with any deviation from his plan.

God demanded a mediator. No one could hope to come into God's presence directly, only indirectly through a priest. And not just anyone could be a priest. A priest had to be a male descendant of Aaron, who was not "blind or lame, disfigured or deformed" (21:18). Even after being set apart by God, this able-bodied priest had to be consecrated by the community through the ritual of ordination. This consecrated priest himself required the mediation of the high priest, the only one permitted into the Most Holy Place, and then only once per year. On that occasion, even he had to come with the blood of a goat and bull and protect himself by filling the room with the smoke of burning incense.

To serve such a demanding Master requires ready and faith-filled obedience. God's will must be done on earth as it is in heaven. Strict obedience is a practical way of honoring God, setting his purposes above all others. The servant's goal is neither to avoid the punishment that follows disobedience nor to reap the blessings of obedience. The goal is to honor God, to treat him as he deserves, whatever it might cost.

One important aspect of honoring God is to allow nothing and no one to take his place. One's loyalty must be undivided. As the

Israelites learned at the foot of Mount Sinai, God would tolerate no other gods in addition to him (see Ex. 32). And as Moses would learn some time later, God would not take it lightly when an opportunity to honor him was lost because of human frustration and a lack of faith (see Num. 20).

Serving such a Master also required good balance. God's gracious provision brought assurance and peace, yet God insisted on being obeyed and was not reticent to make demands. God is demanding, but he is never capricious or greedy. The chief beneficiary of God's demands is not God but his people. God makes precisely this point in Deuteronomy 10:13.

Maintaining the balance between enjoying God's provision and strictly obeying his commands has never been easy. We tend to focus either on God's gracious provision or on his demands. We find it difficult to observe both in equal measure. Some feel the weight of God's expectations so heavily that they lose sight of his promise that he will not give us more than we can carry. Talk of God's immeasurable love rolls off without sinking in. Others delight in God's generosity but forget that he insists on being honored, not for what he gives, but for who he is. When God fails to meet their expectations they are surprised.

CONCLUSION

In addition to describing the deliverance of God's people from Egyptian bondage, the book of Exodus reveals God teaching his people—Moses and the Israelites—what it means to be faithful servants. They understood God's power and how he wanted to employ that power in tandem with his servants. They understood how God provided for their needs and the importance of honoring him through faith-filled obedience.

From Mount Sinai, the Israelites embarked on their journey to Canaan. Though the journey should have taken less than two weeks (see Deut. 1:2), Israel's faith faltered, delaying their entry into the Promised Land by forty years. True to form, God wandered with them, using those years to teach them more about what it meant to be his servants. In particular, Moses would learn hard but valuable lessons about how to serve under fire.

10

Moses under Fire

NUMBERS 11–20

Although Moses' task of leading the Israelites was never easy, a particularly difficult period is described in Numbers 11–20. Moses was faced with repeated challenges to his leadership by leaders from both his own tribe and other tribes, even from his own brother and sister. Some blamed Moses for doing too little; others blamed him for doing too much. Most cries arose because of the spiritual immaturity of God's people. None were fully justified, though at least one sounds as if it has a biblical basis. A careful study of these chapters provides insight into the nature of the challenges faced by God's servants, even today. But more importantly, we discover essential qualities God's servants must possess to face and overcome those challenges.

COMPLAINTS ABOUT PROVISION

You may sense a bit of déjà vu as you read Numbers 11. We've seen something like this earlier in Exodus 16. Just a few days after God had led the Israelites through the Red Sea, they complained about their lack of food. At that time, God responded with a double miracle: the provision of both manna and quail. The provision of quail appears to have been only of brief duration, but the manna had continued every day since, exception the Sabbaths, when God had continued to miraculously preserve Friday's collection.

After a year, the miracle of manna had become mundane. The people no longer took it as bread from heaven; they took it for granted instead. What had begun as a wonder had become commonplace. What had been a gift worth memorializing in the ark of the covenant had become a burden and a source of frustration. This turn of events would be striking were it not so common among God's people. Human nature finds wonder difficult to sustain.

Moses' response to the people's complaints is disappointing, though understandable. He turned to God in prayer—so far so good—but his prayer voiced more frustration than faith (Num. 11:11–15). He blamed God for causing him such trouble, suggesting that a servant of God should get better treatment. He questioned his relationship with God. He even got snarky, wondering what he had done to deserve this treatment and asking if *he* had fathered all these people, a not-so-subtle reminder that the people were God's problem. Moses all but accused God of reneging on his obligations; after all, God had claimed Israel as his firstborn (see Ex. 4:22), complained Moses. God had promised to bring these people to the land (Num. 11:12) but left Moses to do the heavy lifting.

We can understand Moses' frustration; leading the Israelites was harder than most tasks. Yet our sympathies do not change the fact that Moses had stumbled into a very common mistake among God's servants. He overestimated what was asked of him while underestimating God's capabilities. Moses felt obligated to carry those people like a babysitter carries an infant, all the while doubting God's ability to repeat the miracle of providing food. Moses placed himself in a double bind, feeling obligated to become God while seeing God as no stronger than a human. This self-imposed responsibility left Moses feeling helpless; death would have been preferable to this no-win situation, so he thought.

In spite of the fact that Moses misunderstood almost everything about this situation and prayed all the wrong things, God answered. Too kind and good to give Moses what he asked for, God gave him what he needed: help. First, he provided leaders to help Moses bear the weight of the people's demands. It must have felt like both an affirmation and a rebuke that God took from Moses a portion of the Spirit he had been given and passed it on to the seventy leaders. Moses must have felt affirmed that he possessed enough of God's Spirit to share but chagrined to know that with that much of God's Spirit he should have handled the crisis differently.

God provided help of another sort: a second helping of quail. As noted in our discussion of Exodus 16, the migration of quail in the spring is not uncommon in the Sinai wilderness. Here again we have a miracle of timing and scope: God sending the birds at just the right time and in ample measure, mixed with God's gracious provision was the stern reminder that his people needed to trust more and grumble less.

COMPLAINTS ABOUT AUTHORITY

Some of the Israelite grumblers were among Moses' close family. His brother, Aaron, and sister, Miriam, felt it necessary to complain about Moses' Cushite wife (Num. 12:1). This may be another, albeit unusual, way of referring to Zipporah, elsewhere described as being from Midian. Or it may refer to another, hitherto unmentioned, wife. As it turns out, the siblings' issue was not with the wife but with Moses' authority. The mention of Moses' wife may have been a pretense for picking a quarrel with their brother. Or Mrs. Moses may have behaved imperiously toward them—like a queen with her subjects—coloring their view of their brother.

They were family, but this was no ordinary family squabble. As one commentator notes, Aaron was the high priest, and Miriam was a respected prophetess (see Ex. 15:20). Perhaps they felt Moses was usurping authority that belonged to the priests or prophets.[1] Apparently their complaints began outside Moses' hearing, for the text refers to them speaking about Moses, rather than to him: "'Has the LORD spoken only through Moses?' they asked. 'Hasn't he also spoken through us?'" Their complaint may have been unheard by their brother, but "the LORD heard this" (Num. 12:2).

God confronted Aaron and Miriam in the presence of their brother outside the Tent of Meeting (v. 4). While acknowledging the role of prophet as messenger of God, Yahweh put Moses in a class by himself. Prophets may see visions and have dreams, but God spoke to Moses "face to face" (v. 8), or more literally, "mouth to mouth," suggesting close, personal conversation. Although God dwells in light inaccessible, Aaron and Miriam's brother had the privilege of beholding him. How dare they challenge Moses!

Note the criteria God used to extol Moses in verses 6–8. God chose Moses for his servant, and Moses was faithfully executing that role. If Aaron and Miriam's contention was that they should share Moses' authority because they were family, God made it clear that family had nothing to do with it. If they were upset that their priestly and prophetic roles were being neglected, God's correction implied that each should be faithful in the roles to which they were called.

As the cloud representing God's glory lifted from the tent, Aaron saw that Miriam had suddenly become leprous. The Hebrew term used here can describe a variety of skin diseases; in this case, the disease had caused Miriam's skin to turn white. Perhaps God chose this punishment to provide a striking contrast to the blackness of skin associated with Cush (see v. 1). Why Miriam only and not Aaron? Perhaps she was the chief instigator. Another possibility is that both were equally guilty, but inflicting Aaron with leprosy would have left the Israelites without a high priest, something God was too gracious to allow.

Aaron turned immediately to Moses, combining apology with appeal. He referred to his brother as "my lord" and admitted that their complaint was both foolish and sinful (v. 11). Even turning to Moses rather than interceding with God himself demonstrates Aaron's recognition of Moses' true authority. Moses' response was immediate and impassioned: "Please, God, heal her!" (v. 13). God obliged but insisted she remain outside the camp for seven days, an isolation period associated with healing from skin diseases (see Lev. 14:8).

COMPLAINTS OF INCOMPETENCE

The first two controversies pale in comparison with the one engulfing Moses in Numbers 13–14. In response to the Israelites' request (see Deut. 1:22) and with God's permission (Num. 13:1–3), Moses sent twelve spies to explore Canaan. They returned several weeks later with a mixed report: the land was very fruitful but occupied by powerful people, against whom the Israelites would be impotent.

The Israelites were terrified. They realized their vulnerable position: unable to advance and unable to survive in the wilderness without God's help. They now assumed that help would be withdrawn, for either Yahweh's power had failed or the whole exodus had been a divine trick to destroy them. Their only option was to return to Egypt, and they would need a new leader to take them there.

Moses and Aaron responded by falling on their faces (14:5), a gesture implying horror at what the Israelites were suggesting. Having been rescued from Egypt by God's mercy, they now proposed to enslave themselves again, an act of gross ingratitude. The Israelites doubted God's power even though they had witnessed remarkable things, like the parting of the Red Sea and the provision of manna and water. They had been rescued because God had chosen them to be part of his redemptive plan, but they were rejecting that plan and any part of it.

In response to Israel's faithlessness, God expressed his intention to annihilate the Israelites and begin again with Moses (*you* is singular in v. 12), not the first time God had made such an offer (see Ex. 32:10). This had to be tempting: to lead a nation of one's own, greater and stronger than Israel. Such a people would certainly be more manageable, all descendants of Moses, and the number would be miniscule by comparison. Having a nation of his own, Moses would face no more contention over who was in charge.

However tempting this might have seemed, Moses knew (as God himself knew) that such a plan would not work. This is a case where God appears to move in one direction in order to elicit a faith-filled response from his followers in the other direction. Just as Jesus only appeared to refuse the Syrophoenician woman (Mark 7:24–30) and only appeared to be traveling farther as he spoke with his disciples on the road to Emmaus (Luke 24:28), God only appeared intent on destroying Israel.

Instead of taking the easy way, Moses interceded for the people who wanted to replace him—or perhaps do something even worse (Num. 14:13–19). His intercession was for their benefit but not based on their merits. Moses first appealed to God's reputation (vv. 13–16). If Moses' words seem patronizing and unworthy of God, look again. Everything Moses said about God is absolutely true: to change strategy at this point would have cast God in a negative light. To slight God's reputation would be a serious matter, not for the sake of God's ego but for the sake of humanity's well-being. God does not need our praise; he existed from eternity until the creation of the world without human adoration. We are the ones who need to honor God, for we cannot be fully human until we do. This is why we were created—to honor God and enjoy him forever. A right conception of God is our true north; without that, we wander, disoriented.

Moses next appealed to God's character and word (vv. 17–18). God is the perfect balance of grace and justice and responds in proper measure every time. The Israelites had to be punished for their faithlessness, but to destroy the whole nation and begin again would be overkill. The best thing to do, in this instance, would be to forgive them. Moses did not ask that their actions be overlooked, only dealt with in a manner befitting God's perfect blend of love and justice. Moses' confident negotiations with God call to mind Abraham appealing for the righteous in Sodom and Gomorrah (see Gen. 18). God honored the confidence of his appointed leader by acting in accordance with his character, restraining from overreacting but promising appropriate punishment (Num. 14:20–38).

Given Moses' frequent and effective intercessory prayers, it is worth noting that he also knew when not to bother (and even when to pray a prayer of imprecation, as in 16:15). He understood that those who brought this most recent disaster on Israel—the ten spies who saw Canaan but issued a negative report—deserved a more severe punishment. They not only had been personally faithless but had also abused their divinely appointed influence, casting a pall of despair over the people. Leadership is always a two-edged sword, providing the opportunity to magnify one's influence, whether for better or worse. Here, as elsewhere, Moses withheld intercession because the punishment was just.

MORE COMPLAINTS ABOUT AUTHORITY

Numbers 16–17 contain yet another example of Moses' leadership under fire. Two rebellions occurred concurrently, one led by Korah, a Levite, and the other by leaders from the tribe of Reuben (Dathan, Abiram, and On). The former objected to the restriction of priestly activity to the family of Aaron; the latter objected to the elevation of Moses and the tribe of Levi to the exclusion of the tribe of Reuben, Jacob's firstborn son. The fortunes of the Reubenites had been on the decline for centuries, ever since their forefather had slept with Bilhah, one of his father's concubines (see Gen. 35:22;

49:3–4). Other tribes emerged as more significant, particularly Levi in regard to the sanctuary and Judah in regard to leadership (see Num. 10:14).

The specific complaint of Dathan and Abiram is stated in Numbers 16:12–14. They rejected Moses' authority over them because they felt he had failed in his responsibilities. He had taken the people from a wonderful land but failed to bring them into a better one, leaving them to die in the wilderness. Ironies abound in their words. Moses had summoned them, presumably to join the others at the entrance to the tent, but the rebels had refused to go (vv. 12, 14). They had previously been invited by God, through Caleb, to go and enter Canaan (13:30). Now they wouldn't even go to the tent to see what God had to say. They referred to Egypt as a land flowing with milk and honey, apparently forgetting they had been slaves in that land. The phrase they used for Egypt is better applied to the land of Canaan (see 14:8), the land they had just rejected as too dangerous to enter. Moses had not failed to lead them to Canaan; he had brought the nation to the very border of that land. They had failed to enter due to their lack of faith in God. They spoke of Moses as depriving them of their inheritance. God had promised them Canaan as their inheritance, but they, not Moses, had spurned it as surely as Esau had spurned his birthright. Their final complaint, that Moses wanted to "treat these men like slaves" (16:14), could be rendered more literally as "put out the eyes of these men" (NASB). The New International Version may be right to treat this as an idiom, but this is abject slavery, like that imposed on Samson when captured by the Philistines (see Judg. 16:21).

Korah was not merely a Levite; he was from the clan of the Kohathites, those charged with transporting the sanctuary furniture, including the ark of the covenant (Num. 3:31). He was not the leader of this clan but proved sufficiently persuasive to enlist the support of 250 leaders of Israel (16:2). We do not know their tribal affiliation; they may have been Levites or may have represented other tribes as well.

Their complaint had some legitimacy. God had declared all the Israelites a "kingdom of priests and a holy nation" (Ex. 19:6). Why then, they demanded, should only Aaron and his sons be able to fulfill that role? All should have equal access to God, they insisted, a demand that resonates with our North American egalitarian preferences. Korah could even point to the blue thread in the tassels on every Israelite robe, for these demonstrate that all Israel had been consecrated to God (Num. 15:37–41).

In God's design, however, all would be holy, but not all would be equally holy. From the holy nation, God chose the Levites to be holier than the other eleven tribes. From the Levites, God chose one family to be holier than others; and from this family, God chose one man—the high priest—to be holier than all. Although they addressed their complaint to both Moses and Aaron (*you* in 16:3 is plural), it more directly targets Aaron. Korah and the others understood that Moses had set this hierarchical plan in place, privileging his brother. What they failed to understand is that Moses did so in obedience to God's direction. This hierarchical design did not fit Korah's paradigm for what was best; he used God's own words to support his claim, but he was still wrong. He failed to acknowledge and appreciate God's revealed and useful design. Moses understood that Korah's motivation was not for equality but self-advancement. Having already received the great privilege of being a Levite, he was now "trying to get the priesthood too" (v. 10). Korah's argument illustrates how easily Scripture can be used against itself by one whose goal is not honoring God.

Moses' solution was to let God decide. All contestants would bring censers and bronze containers holding coals and engage in the priestly task of burning incense before Yahweh. As with any king, entry to God's presence was by invitation only; the uninvited entered at their own risk. The "one" (v. 7) who survived (Moses already knew what the outcome would be) would be the man God had chosen.

As the challengers gathered at the entrance to the tent, God proposed an alternative plan: He would destroy the whole "assembly" (v. 21). This may refer to just those who had challenged Moses and Aaron (vv. 5–6, 11, 16, 19) but more likely refers to the entire nation. The same Hebrew term is used in verse 2 in reference to the group from which the 250 leaders came ("well-known community leaders" could instead by rendered "princes from the assembly"). The word is also used several times in this chapter to describe the whole nation of Israel (vv. 3, 9, 19, 24, 26).

Moses once again interceded and once again appealed to God's reputation and character. By referring to God as the "God of the spirits of all flesh" (v. 22 ESV), Moses likely referred to Yahweh's role as the righteous judge, the only one with the authority to give or take life. God was too just to wipe out the entire nation for the sins of a small portion of that nation, that small portion referred to here poetically as "one man" (v. 22).

Once again, God answered Moses' prayer, sparing the entire nation and taking the lives of only a few. The 250 men who presumed to enter God's presence were killed (v. 35). So too were Korah, Dathan, and Abiram (no mention is made of On, son of Peleth, though he was probably destroyed too). The manner in which the men were killed reinforced Moses' divine sanction: the ground opened up and swallowed the households of the rebels.

While it does not fit our definition of fairness to punish the families of the guilty men, we must read this in light of the culture in which this incident took place. It was widely assumed that one's guilt was shared by the entire household. The expectation was, in the words of one ancient Near Eastern document, "Whoever has disobeyed has no family, has nothing alive." One of the pharaohs wrote in a letter to a territorial governor, "But if you perform your service for the king, your lord, what is there that the king will not do for you? If for any reason whatsoever you prefer to do evil, and if you plot evil, treacherous things, then you, together with your entire family, shall die by the axe of the king."[2]

Even though Moses had spared the nation from widespread punishment, the people complained about God's severity. In response, Yahweh began a slow but steady purging of his people. Only Moses' quick intercession and Aaron's courage limited the death toll. As the judgment on Korah, Dathan, and Abiram had demonstrated Moses' authority, so the sparing of the Israelites through Aaron's actions confirmed his divine appointment as high priest, chief intermediary between God and humanity.

Numbers 17 further confirms that point. There we read that God clearly confirmed Aaron as his choice for priest. Aaron's rod not only sprouted leaves but also "budded, blossomed, and produced ripe almonds" (v. 8 NLT)! As if to preempt further debate on this same point, Aaron's staff was to be kept inside the Most Holy Place so it could be presented as undeniable proof. Numbers 18–19 focuses on the responsibilities of the priests and Levites, those divinely sanctioned to approach Yahweh on behalf of his people.

GOD'S SERVANT UNDER FIRE

Being a faithful servant of God did not insulate Moses from the fires of controversy. He often found himself caught in the middle, between his Master and those over whom he had been appointed. What made Moses a faithful servant is that he remembered where his ultimate loyalty lay. He was God's servant first and foremost; what he did for God's people was done on God's behalf.

The challenges he faced ran the spectrum, some people claiming he did too little, and others that he did too much. The former criticized him for failing to adequately provide for their needs and failing to bring them to a better place. The latter criticized him for being too authoritarian. The Israelites are not the only people who have been hard to please and easily misled, and Moses was not the last of God's servants to discover the less appealing side of God's saints.

Moses provides a good example, however, of what it takes to serve God under such circumstances. First, one must be humble. A later inspired hand (not likely Moses himself), described Moses as "a very humble man, more humble than anyone on the face of the earth" (12:3). This is not a randomly placed endorsement; this description of Moses demonstrates that the complaint of Aaron and Miriam was baseless. It also provides an admiring assessment of how Moses dealt with challenges to his leadership. By leading in a self-effacing manner, he weakened any accusation that he was building his own kingdom or feathering his own nest. Even Moses' humility did not protect him from such accusations, but it did limit them and blunt their effect.

Furthermore, exercising humility is the right way to handle such accusations. Human nature is likely to rise to its own defense at such moments; humility moderates the temptation to make ourselves appear better than we are and to make our accusers seem worse than they might be. Responding with humility allows God's servants to see the legitimacy in any accusation and make the appropriate adjustments. Moses' humility allowed him to share leadership with the seventy elders. Remember how he responded when Joshua arrived with the potentially threatening news that Eldad and Medad were also prophesying. "Are you jealous for my sake? I wish that all the LORD's people were prophets and that the LORD would put his Spirit on them" (11:29). Only a humble person makes a wish like that.

Moses' humility also enabled him to keep a clear perspective. Amid the fire of controversy, smoke can cloud one's vision. Moses knew the nation was ready to replace him after the spies delivered their report, but his eyes were not on his own future but on God's glory. This enabled Moses to make an effective appeal. He saw through Korah's request, understanding that while there was some theological validity to the demands, the real issue lay elsewhere — inside Korah's power-hungry heart.

Humility, once attained, can be set aside. Such was the case for Moses in still another moment of testing. Numbers 20 describes the Israelites complaining once again about the lack of water. God instructed Moses how to provide water, even directing him to take *the* staff — likely Aaron's staff, which was kept in the Most Holy Place — and go to the rock. In an earlier confrontation with thirsty Israelites, God had instructed Moses to strike the rock (see Ex. 17), but this time he was only to speak to it.

He did not speak to the rock but to the people, and his words had an ominous stridency to them, referring to the Israelites as "rebels." We hear more of Moses than of God in these words: "Must we bring you water from this rock?" (Num. 20:10). Moses then struck the rock, not once but twice.

Water came out, but so did a strong remonstrance from God. He accused Moses and Aaron of failing to trust him, of missing an opportunity to honor God before the Israelites. The offense may seem small to us, too insignificant to merit such a severe punishment. That is because we underestimate the value of seeing God reveal himself more clearly. We were made to know him; to be deprived of an opportunity to do so is no small thing.

MOSES UNDER FIRE

For Moses, this may have been a moment of carelessness. God had told him to strike a rock before and bring the same staff with him on this occasion. Moses may have thought he could do the same thing again and get the same result. He would not be the last of God's servants in an unguarded moment to think of God more like a machine than a personal being. Or Moses may have reached a tipping point in his dealings with the grumblers. His tone and words sound as if he was exasperated. Whether his actions resulted from carelessness or frustration, humility would have provided the needed protection, heightening his attention to God's instructions and tempering his mood with a reminder of his own humanity.

That dark moment aside, Moses modeled a second quality that is most helpful when God's servants endure the fire, a strong trust in God. This trust explains why Moses so quickly turned to God in prayer. As demonstrated by his words in Numbers 11:11–15, 21–22, Moses' prayers were not always on target, but at least they were honest words directed to his only source of help. Moses' trust in God also clarifies the point at which intercession is fruitless. At times Moses prayed for God to spare the guilty; at other times he remained silent, allowing punishment to come (see 11:33; 14:36–37, 44–45; 16:31–35).

Moses trusted God to defend him against his enemies, whether Canaanite or Israelite. He trusted God's wisdom and guidance, relying on God's Spirit (see Num. 11:17). God's servant continued to trust, even when the Master's wisdom seemed mistaken. If Moses wondered whether God should have permitted the spies to be sent, he never let on. Even though the outcome was disastrous, Moses remained fully committed to what God had commanded.

Moses trusted also in God's ability to work miracles, such as opening the ground to swallow Korah and company. There were times when Moses' confidence in God's power barely kept up with the challenges, moments when he wondered whether God's arm was, in fact, too short (vv. 21–23). But all it took for Moses' confidence to catch up was hearing God's simple promise: "Now you will see" (v. 23).

Moses' faith is evident in his recognition of the importance of God's presence. When the Israelites purposed to take on the Canaanites on their own, Moses warned of the disaster that would follow: "Do not go up, because the LORD is not with you. You will be defeated by your enemies. . . . Because you have turned away from the LORD, he will not be with you and you will fall by the sword" (14:42–43).

The events of Numbers 15 occur amid these chapters describing God's servant under fire. Though at first glance it appears out of place, dealing as it does with various kinds of offerings and tassels on Israelite robes, this chapter is strategically located to emphasize the dual themes of humility and trust. Moses and the Israelites had to demonstrate the humility required to obey God's laws concerning the Sabbath, even taking the responsibility to judge and punish those who disobeyed. They were required to recognize the seriousness of all sin, even unintentional sin, and provide the requisite offerings. Most serious of all was intentional sin, committed by those who despise Yahweh's word and break his command. This person sins "defiantly" (v. 30), or more literally, "with a high hand," a Hebrew idiom for pride.

But God's servants could have confidence that God would keep his promise to bring them to Canaan. Note what God instructed Moses to say to the Israelites: "After you enter the land I am giving you as a home" (v. 2). The people had rebelled, initiated plans to return to Egypt, threatened the leaders of their people, and engaged in an unsanctioned attack on Canaan. And still God spoke of the time "after" they entered the land he would give them. God's grace always provides forgiveness and a second chance for those who trust him.

Both trust and humility are represented in the law about tassels (vv. 37–41). Within each tassel is a blue cord, the only purpose of which was to remind the Israelites that they belonged to Yahweh. As his covenant people, they needed to humbly obey his commands, whether as small as wearing a tassel or as large as exercising capital punishment. As Yahweh's covenant people, they could trust that the God who brought them out of Egypt would remain faithful.

CONCLUSION

The book of Numbers concludes with the Israelites at the border of Canaan, poised to enter. Before they did, God wanted to make his expectations for his people very clear, so they paused for an extended reminder. We know this reminder as the book of Deuteronomy. God also wanted to bring about a change in leadership, appointing Joshua to lead Israel in the next leg of the journey and allowing Moses to conclude his faithful service with the dignity and honor he deserved.

11

Faithful to the End: Moses and the New Generation

DEUTERONOMY 1–34

Moses, a faithful servant of God, had come to the end of his earthly service to his heavenly Master. In his words and actions, he demonstrated faithfulness to the very end, quite literally, though that end was not without challenges of its own. Moses' faithful service in this case was not demonstrated by working miracles or encountering God on the mountain but by carefully reminding the Israelites of their responsibility to be faithful servants themselves after he was gone. Moses reinforced for the Israelites a proper understanding of their God and themselves. He also revealed what was to come and what God would require of them as it came.

KNOW GOD

Explicit statements about God's character are made throughout the books of Exodus, Leviticus, and Numbers, but the frequency of those statements increases in the book of Deuteronomy. As his years of service drew to a close, Moses appeared especially concerned that the Israelites should know the full truth about God.

The picture that appears more regularly than all others in Deuteronomy is God as father. In the opening chapter, Moses compares God's deliverance of the Israelites to a father carrying his son (1:31). I think back to those days when my son, now a man, was just a boy. When his little legs couldn't keep my grown-up pace or he had become too exhausted to take another step, he would stop and lift his arms toward me. It then became my happy privilege to hoist him onto my hip, let him ride piggy-back, or let him sit on my shoulders while I did the walking for both of us. God chose this picture of a father carrying his child to describe how he had delivered his people. They could not keep up with the lightning pace at which their deliverance came; their legs were weary, slavery having allowed few opportunities for lengthy journeys. So God carried them, doing the walking for both of them.

As beautiful as this picture of God's paternal affection is, it must be viewed alongside the rest of what we learn about God from Deuteronomy. This father is a heavenly Father, the One to whom "the secret things belong" (29:29), the One who judged the Israelites in the wilderness, who demanded their full obedience, who controls the destiny of all nations. "To the LORD your God belong the heavens, even the highest heavens, the earth and everything in it. Yet the LORD set his affection on your ancestors and loved them, and he chose you, their descendants, above all the nations—as it is today" (10:14–15). We must remember both God's paternal closeness and his sovereign otherness if we are to be in relationship with him.

God treated the Israelites in the wilderness as a father treats his child. He provided needed resources but also allowed opportunities for the child to grow and mature. The people needed food, so their heavenly Father gave them manna from heaven. They also needed to learn to trust God on a daily basis, so God gave them the manna in daily doses, with a double supply on the day before the Sabbath. In this way, he proved and improved the quality of their faith. "The LORD your God is testing you," said Moses, "to find out whether you love him with all your heart and with all your soul" (13:3). Because he is omniscient, God already knows the condition of our hearts; when he tests us, those tests are meant to demonstrate the truth so that we can know it as well.

When the Israelites disobeyed, their heavenly Father disciplined them. Moses wanted them to understand that the hardships they had experienced in their travels were not evidence of God's distance but of his closeness. "Know then in your heart that as a man disciplines his son, so the LORD your God disciplines you" (8:5). Like any good father, God is jealous for his children's love. Moses warned the people away from idolatry: "For the LORD your God, who is among you, is a jealous God and his anger will burn against you" (6:15). God's jealousy arises, not from his own need but from the awareness that love is evidence of health. When a child fails to love his or her parent or fails to show that love in respectful and appropriate ways, something has gone wrong. The problem may be traceable to mistakes made by the parent, by the child, or both. Either way, something is amiss. It is even more serious when God's children fail to love their heavenly Father, betraying him and living contrary to his clear instructions.

God loves us too much to allow such a condition to persist. His jealousy compels him to intervene, usually by punishment. God's punishment is always purposeful, intended to get our attention and restore a proper relationship. Shortly after describing God as "a consuming fire, a jealous God" (4:24), Moses referred to Yahweh as "merciful," one who would "not abandon or destroy [his children] or forget the covenant [he had made] with [their] ancestors, which he confirmed to them by oath" (4:31). Elsewhere Moses described this perfect balance of divine jealousy and mercy this way: "Know therefore that the LORD your God is God; he is the faithful God, keeping his covenant of love to a thousand generations of those who love him and keep his commandments. But those who hate him he will repay to their face by destruction; he will not be slow to repay to their face those who hate him" (7:9–10).

KNOW YOURSELVES

To know God as one's heavenly Father requires knowing oneself as his child. Without both, the knowledge of either is deficient. In Deuteronomy 1–3, Moses not only identified the Israelites as sons (and, by implication, daughters) of God but also reinforced this relationship by retelling Israel's history. Curiously, the history does not begin with Abraham or even the burning bush. Nothing is said of the dramatic plagues or the parting of the Red Sea. Instead, Moses began the story at Sinai and described that generation's more recent history. In particular, he related Israel's recent interactions with God, including their selection of leaders, the disastrous events surrounding the twelve spies, the resultant wanderings, the defeat of the Amorite kings Sihon and Og and the distribution of their land, and Moses' own failure.

Moses' choice of material suggests that he sought to reveal particular aspects of Israel's identity for particular purposes. Some of these stories reveal Israelite failures, especially their fearful refusal to enter the land (1:19—2:23). Even Moses himself had the clay feet common to humanity (3:21–29). It may have been hard to hear, but the Israelites needed to be reminded of their disobedience.

FAITHFUL TO THE END: MOSES AND THE NEW GENERATION

Moses' purpose in sharing this depressing truth was to provide the proper diagnosis for these setbacks. The Israelites were neither unlucky nor cursed nor inadequate; they were disobedient. That sounds like bad news but is actually good news. For the Israelites, it was something like receiving a sobering diagnosis from a doctor. The news was scary, but at least the right diagnosis clarified the proper treatment and put them on the path to healing. Knowing the painful truth about themselves made it possible for Israel to experience the blessings of obedience.

Many of the stories in this history lesson are not about Israel's failures but are reminders of how God brought them success. As the people faithfully obeyed, God brought victory over the enemy (2:24—3:20). With victory came extra land, land not originally part of God's intended territory. How like God to reward faithfulness with a full cup, pressed down, shaken together, running over.

One of the history lessons described in these chapters is how God provided leaders when Moses' resources were stretched thin (1:9–18). This story describes not only God's provision of leaders but also the population growth that made additional leaders necessary. Because of God's blessing, the Israelites were now "as numerous as the stars in the sky" (1:10).

The overall emphasis in the stories Moses chose to include in this review of Israel's history is Israel's propensity to disobey and God's gracious provision when they remain faithful. This was what they needed to know about themselves. To hear only of their faithlessness would have left them in despair, but failing to know their true condition would have doomed them to the illusion of success. To know both their true condition without God and their amazing potential with him offered the greatest hope of blessing.

Moses summarized Israel's true nature this way: "You are the children of the LORD your God" (14:1). Like children, they were prone to stumble; that is what happens when someone is learning to walk. Having spent centuries without a clear knowledge of God, learning to walk by faith took time and practice. The Israelites were, however, God's children. Joined in a covenant relationship with their heavenly Father, they had the tremendous blessing of his presence and direction. They also had the potential of rich blessings, so long as they lived faithfully to his expectations for them.

KNOW WHAT GOD EXPECTS OF YOU

God's expectations for his children are clear: "Love the LORD your God with all your heart and with all your soul and with all your strength" (6:5). How appropriate that *love* is the most important word to define our relationship with God. He is our Father, and we are his children. The verb translated "love" expresses the affection, commitment, and loyalty appropriate for such a relationship. This is the term used to describe Abraham's love for Isaac (Gen. 22:2) and Jacob's love for Joseph (37:3). We must be careful, however, not to misread what God meant by loading this term with contemporary connotations that do not fit its ancient meaning. When we speak of love, we put most of the emphasis on the strong and positive emotion we feel. The Hebrew term can include such emotion (see 24:67) but places greater emphasis on the commitment produced by that love. Those who love things like food and wine demonstrate that love by eating and drinking. Those who love others demonstrate that love by their commitment to do good to those people. Ruth loved her mother-in-law by committing herself to Naomi's well-being (Ruth 4:15). Jonathan loved David by making a covenant with him and honoring that agreement even when it put him at odds with his own father (1 Sam. 18:3). Hiram, king of Tyre, loved David and expressed that love by being loyal to David's son, Solomon (1 Kings 5:1).

The most significant demonstration of love for another person is loyalty. To love God with the entirety of one's heart, soul, and strength means to be completely loyal to God and to show that loyalty through actions. Feelings are not irrelevant, but they are no substitute for loyal behavior.

Moses made clear to the Israelites that the specifics of such loving, loyal behavior were given in the law he had received from God on Mount Sinai. Another way of describing that law is to wholeheartedly love God and one's neighbor. As stated earlier, the first half of the Ten Commandments focuses on what it means to love God, the second half focuses on what it means to love one's neighbor.

As the first five commandments suggest, in order to love God properly one must worship him properly. In his final instructions, Moses returned to this topic. The Israelites were to worship Yahweh in the proper place and worship him properly in that place. Israel would be tempted to worship wherever they thought was an appropriately sacred space, since this had been the practice of the surrounding nations. God had apparently permitted such freedom in the past, and to worship at the place of one's own choosing would have been easier than trekking to a single sanctuary. But when the Israelites finally arrived at their destination, they were to destroy all other sanctuaries, come to the one place where God would choose to put his name, and bring all the specified offerings. This sanctuary was to be a place of joy and fellowship (Deut. 12:2–27). The Israelites were to eat the proper foods, prepared in the proper way, in order to remain eligible to worship God (14:1–21). They would also have to tithe so that those required to lead them in worship would be provided for (12:19; 14:22–29; 18:1–13). Also, all the sacred festivals would have to be observed (16:1–17). Israel must worship properly, said Moses, "So that it may always go well with you and your children after you, because you will be doing what is good and right in the eyes of the LORD your God" (12:28).

In Deuteronomy, Moses put great emphasis on the importance of avoiding idolatry. The inhabitants of Canaan had many unsavory qualities, but the one most often criticized was their worship of other gods. No hint of idolatry was to be tolerated among the Israelites. Anyone who even suggested the practice was to be killed, even if it was one's own sibling, child, spouse, or friend. Anyone who offered secret enticement, saying, "Let us go and worship other gods" (13:6), should be shown no mercy. Moses instructed, "Show them no pity. Do not spare them or shield them. You must certainly put them to death. Your hand must be the first in putting them to death, and then the hands of all the people" (v. 9; see also 16:21—17:7).

Moses' great fear was not that the Israelites would completely forsake Yahweh and worship another god. Examples of that in the Old Testament are rare. Syncretism, or the worship of another god alongside Yahweh, was far more likely. This is what Moses warned against, for example, when he prohibited the erection of a wooden Asherah pole or sacred stone "beside the altar you build to the LORD your God" (16:21). The Asherah pole and stone were used for the worship of other gods (7:5); these should have no place anywhere in Israel, least of all alongside God's altar.

Loving God required the Israelites to obey the law of Moses, but the law also laid down clear requirements for the treatment of one's neighbor. In other words, loving God wholeheartedly required treating others fairly too. The law required the forgiveness of debts and liberation of servants every seven years to help people avoid poverty (15:1–4, 12–15, 18). Should some become poor, the Israelites were not to be "hardhearted or tightfisted toward them.

Rather . . . openhanded and freely lend them whatever they need" (15:7–8). Judges and law courts were to be established to ensure justice (16:18–20; 17:8–13). Women, even foreign captives, were not to be abused (21:10–14; 22:13–19). Human dignity and property rights were to be maintained, as were strict rules regarding honesty (19:14–21; 22:1–4; 24:6–15; 25:13–16). Even the king should not imagine himself above the law (17:14–20).

Avoiding idolatry and treating one's neighbor fairly are essential elements in loving God wholeheartedly. No wonder these were the two accusations leveled against God's people most often by later prophets. The faithful servant must protect his or her Master's honor by absolute loyalty and by showing concern for the well-being of his or her fellow servants.

Some scholars assume that God's purpose in giving the Israelites the law was to show them that they could not keep it. They view the law as intentionally designed to produce frustration so that God's people would then be willing and able to accept God's offer of grace, which came later through Christ. As noted earlier, nothing could be further from the how Old Testament believers viewed the law. They delighted in it, as evidenced in passages like Psalm 19:7–14 and Psalm 119. They did not find the law a source of frustration but a cause for celebration.

This attitude is also apparent in Moses' words in Deuteronomy. To obey the law demonstrates "wisdom and understanding to the nations, who will hear about all these decrees and say, 'Surely this great nation is a wise and understanding people'" (4:6). No other nation had been given the privilege to hear from God as the Israelites had. And Moses asked, "What other nation is so great as to have such righteous decrees and laws as this body of laws I am setting before you today?" (4:8).

The details of the law might be hard for us to keep straight, but they would not have been hard for the Israelites to keep. "Now what

I am commanding you today," said Moses, "is not too difficult for you or beyond your reach. It is not up in heaven, so that you have to ask, 'Who will ascend into heaven to get it and proclaim it to us so we may obey it?' Nor is it beyond the sea, so that you have to ask, 'Who will cross the sea to get it and proclaim it to us so we may obey it?' No, the word is very near you; it is in your mouth and in your heart so you may obey it" (30:11–14).

One of the ways God made the law more understandable was by building into it the principle of retribution into it. According to this principle, obedience brings blessing while disobedience brings disaster. This principle is described throughout Deuteronomy, especially in passages like 30:15–18 and 28:1–68. It is also demonstrated throughout Israel's history. When the Israelites obeyed God, he blessed them with deliverance, provision, leadership, and everything else they needed. When they disobeyed, disaster struck.

God did not wait until the coming of Christ to reveal his grace. Old Testament believers came into a relationship with God by grace through faith, just as New Testament believers do. As Paul made clear, God chose Abraham before asking Abraham to be circumcised (see Rom. 4). The Israelites did not become God's people by keeping the law. It was because they already were God's people that God rescued them from Egypt, a rescue that preceded the giving of the law on Mount Sinai. Moses made this crystal clear in Deuteronomy 7:7–8. God did not choose the Israelites because of their size or importance. No, as Moses put it, "It was because the LORD loved [them] and kept the oath he swore to [their] ancestors that he brought [them] out with a mighty hand and redeemed [them] from the land of slavery, from the power of Pharaoh king of Egypt" (7:8).

God's expectations for Israel are beautifully summarized in Deuteronomy 10:12–22. The Israelites were to fear and love Yahweh, demonstrating this through faith-filled obedience. They were to worship him and no other, for he is "God of gods and Lord of lords" (v. 17), and they were to treat even the weakest among them—the fatherless, widow, and alien—with compassion, generosity and fairness. This obedience would have to move beyond mere outward adherence to sincere inward commitment. The Israelites were not only to circumcise their bodies but also their hearts. All these commands were given not to satisfy Yahweh's needs but for Israel's "own good" (v. 13).

KNOW WHAT IS TO COME

Moses demonstrated faithful service in yet another way, by providing an honest assessment of Israel's future. The people needed to know the coming opportunities and challenges so they could take full advantage of the former and not be devastated by the latter. Throughout Deuteronomy, Moses revealed three aspects of what laid ahead for God's people: the conquest of the land, the temptation to disobey, and a change in leadership.

The Israelites already knew they were to enter Canaan, but Deuteronomy reveals additional details of what this would mean. They would be given the opportunity to possess territory but only insofar as they dispossessed those now in residence. Much of that would happen without bloodshed as God frightened away the Canaanites by driving them out (see 4:38; 7:22; 9:4–5; 11:23; 18:12; 33:27). Those who refused to leave, however, would have to be removed by force, Israel's force. That God promised to do most of the heavy lifting in the conquest did not alter the fact that unless the Israelites took up their swords, God would not fight for them.

Allowing the Canaanites to remain in the land was not an option, for their influence would be harmful. Those who refused to leave or surrender were to be shown no mercy and totally destroyed (7:2). That sounds harsh, but what was the alternative? The Israelites could not keep a large number of prisoners of war, especially when they would be the very Canaanites most intent on continuing their idolatrous and immoral lifestyle. Israel could not hope to remain faithful to its mission by allowing this sort of influence to remain among its people. As Moses said, "They will turn your children away from following [Yahweh] to serve other gods, and the LORD's anger will burn against you and will quickly destroy you" (7:4).

The Israelites were to deal even more severely with any instance of idolatry among their fellow Israelites. When dealing with Canaanite towns, confiscation of goods and rebuilding could follow destruction. Not so with idolatrous Israelite towns. In those instances, all the property had to be destroyed, and the town was to "remain a ruin forever, never to be rebuilt" (13:16).

Moses provided a second glimpse into Israel's future, and this description is more discouraging. Moses predicted that Israel would turn away from God and suffer the consequences of disobedience (see 31:15—32:47). The tone of God's Word is actually less desperate than it sounds. Ancient Hebrew culture allowed warnings against failure to be stated as predictions of failure. We see something similar in Joshua's parting words to the Israelites (see Josh. 24:19). Israel would later stumble and suffer defeat, but the people had these words to fall back on, explaining the cause for their disasters and the way back to blessing.

Moses' third glimpse of the future concerned the transition to new leadership. Moses had forfeited his right to lead the people into Canaan by striking rather than speaking to the rock in order to produce water. Even though God had clearly stated that Moses would be replaced by Joshua, who would lead the people into Canaan, Moses appealed strongly and repeatedly for a second chance. Although he had failed to honor God by trusting him, his appeal was filled with honor and confidence in God's strength. Moses had witnessed what God had begun to do, so he asked to be able to see the "good land"— the evidence that God's promises had been fulfilled (Deut. 3:23–24). Moses' appeal had been strong and repeated; God's response was also strong but singular: "That is enough" (3:26).

Moses accepted God's decision and helped the Israelites transition to a new leader. In answer to his intercession for the right person, God pointed to Joshua. Moses then formally appointed his lieutenant to succeed him, by means of a ritual conducted before the high priest and people (Num. 27:15–23). The events described in Deuteronomy 31:7–8 could be either that same appointment ritual or a reaffirmation of this decision.

In addition to appointing Joshua, Moses helped prepare the Israelites for the day when Joshua, too, would be gone. One way he did that was to anticipate the time when the Israelites would choose a king and detail the qualities of a good monarch (17:14–20). A second way Moses assisted in the transition of leadership was by writing down the law he had received on Mount Sinai and insisting that it be read to the people regularly and by the king daily (17:19–20; 27:2–3; 31:9–13, 24–26). By making the written law the standard for behavior, Moses gave the people a way to evaluate the quality of their leaders.

Moses helped in the transition of leadership in yet a third way, by opening the minds of the people to the possibility that God would send them a prophet (18:14–22). Other peoples had ways of hearing from their gods, whether through prophecy, sorcery, divination, or consultation with the dead. Israel was privileged to have a leader who spoke with God face-to-face, but that leader-prophet was about to die. God assured them that he would continue to make his will known. They had the law, but they would also hear from prophets who would guide them. From that point on, God chose spokespersons, women and men like Deborah, Samuel, Nathan, Elijah, Elisha, Isaiah, Jeremiah, and many more. Little could anyone then have known how God would fulfill that promise by sending his own Son (see Acts 3:22–26).

KNOW AND MAKE IT KNOWN

It is tempting for those of us who preach and teach to assume that just because we've said something, people have heard it. Sadly, that is not always the case. Moses not only spoke these words to the people but also took steps to ensure they would would hear and remember. He knew that faithful service to his Master required more than merely discharging his obligations; it included doing all he could to ensure that faithful service continued in a new generation. So Moses challenged the current generation of Israelites to take his words to heart. God had made his covenant with their ancestors—Abraham, Isaac, and Jacob—and reaffirmed it with their parents at Mount Sinai, but all those people had died. Moses affirmed that this covenant was not simply a thing of the past but had been made "with us, with all of us who are alive here today" (Deut. 5:3). To reinforce this truth, Moses prescribed a personal ritual. After the people arrived at their destination and reaped the blessings of Canaan, they were to bring the first of their harvest to the sanctuary, present it to the priest, and recite these words:

FAITHFUL TO THE END: MOSES AND THE NEW GENERATION

> My father was a wandering Aramean, and he went down into Egypt with a few people and lived there and became a great nation, powerful and numerous. But the Egyptians mistreated us and made us suffer, subjecting us to harsh labor. Then we cried out to the LORD, the God of our ancestors, and the LORD heard our voice and saw our misery, toil and oppression. So the LORD brought us out of Egypt with a mighty hand and an outstretched arm, with great terror and with signs and wonders. He brought us to this place and gave us this land, a land flowing with milk and honey; and now I bring the firstfruits of the soil that you, LORD, have given me. (26:5–10)

Through this ritual, God's covenant would become more personal to each Israelite.

Moses further insisted that the current generation intentionally make the law known to future generations. They were to impress the importance of these commandments on their children, teach them how to obey, talk about them at every opportunity, and even write them on the doorway of their homes (6:4–9; 11:18–21; 32:46). Every seven years they were to read the law aloud to the Israelites: "Their children, who do not know this law, must hear it and learn to fear the LORD your God as long as you live in the land you are crossing the Jordan to possess" (31:13).

In addition to commanding the current generation to embrace the law and encourage future generations to do the same, Moses employed several other strategies to increase the likelihood that his message would be heard and remembered. One strategy was to expound upon each of the Ten Commandments—the heart of the Mosaic law. As recorded in Deuteronomy 5, Moses repeated the commandments, then explained what it meant to keep them. He explained God's prohibition against having any other gods before him and against worshiping images in chapters 6–11 and chapter 12, respectively. He provided greater clarity to the commands to respect God's name (13:1—14:21), to observe the Sabbath (14:22—16:17), and to honor parents and other human authorities (16:18—18:22). He explained more about the prohibitions against murder (19:1—21:23), adultery (22:1—23:14), theft (23:15—24:7), false testimony (24:8–16), and covetousness (24:17—26:15).[1]

Another strategy is revealed by the structure of Deuteronomy. In the ancient Near East, treaties between nations were often designed in six parts. They began with an introduction or preamble, then, second, contained a historical prologue. Third, they described the agreement, first in general terms and then more specifically. Fourth, these treaties identified where the treaty was to be stored and how it would be disclosed. The fifth part described the blessings that accrued to those who obeyed the terms and the disaster that would come to those who did not. Finally, the treaties described the witnesses.

Deuteronomy unfolds in this six-part fashion. After the introduction (1:1–5), there are several chapters describing the relationship between Yahweh and Israel (1:6—3:29). The general stipulations (5:1—11:32) are followed by detailed stipulations (12:1—26:19). Next are directions about storing the treaty (31:24–26) and about declaring it (27:2–3; 31:9–13). Chapter 28 is devoted to the blessings for obedience and curses for disobedience, while the witnesses are referred to in chapters 31–32. The form in which a message is delivered can either strengthen or weaken its impact. A proposal of marriage might be delivered via text message, but the recipient would not be wise to accept it. Moses chose the right format to present his message because both the form and the content emphasized the importance of reaffirming the covenant.

Still another strategy Moses employed to ensure that his listeners heard and remembered his words was to summarize the message in a song that the Israelites were to memorize (31:19—32:47). Something powerful happens when music and memory combine. Just a phrase or a combination of notes can summon the full score and all the verses, recalling strong emotions. Some who suffer from dementia have trouble remembering what they ate for lunch but can still sing the hymns they learned as children. Recent scholarly literature confirms the potency of music combined with memory.[2] The early church put its theology to music, as evident in passages like Philippians 2:5–11; 1 Timothy 3:16; and 2 Timothy 2:11–13.

Moses wanted his message to be heard, remembered, and embraced. While Israel's later record of obedience is less than stellar, the survival of God's chosen people remains a commendable example of faithfulness under fire. What came to be know as Judaism survived in spite of Assyrian and Babylonian invasion, Persian domination, and Greek attempts at extermination. It was the womb from which Christianity emerged, so we have special reason to applaud its resoluteness and resilience, due in large measure to Moses and the words recorded here. Read the book of Joshua closely and you will hear the strains of Deuteronomy's music. The discovery of the book of the law, likely Deuteronomy, inspired Josiah's reforms of Judah in the seventh century BC. Deuteronomy was one of the most popular books in the community of Jewish monks that gathered in the Judean wilderness at Qumran. And is the third-most-quoted book in the New Testament, after Psalms and Isaiah, appearing in the Gospels, Acts, and the Epistles.

Ironically, one of the first things revealed early in Exodus about the adult Moses was that he had trouble speaking. At the end of his life, however, he spoke and sang words whose eloquence and profundity have echoed through the millennia, producing courage and faithfulness in others. Being a faithful servant appears to be less about one's ability and more about one's availability.

CONCLUSION

Having faithfully completed his service to his Master, Moses died and was buried. Even at the graveside, we learn more of what it means to be God's faithful servant. The work of the servant concludes at God's say-so, not the servant's. Moses wanted to continue leading the people and had the strength to do so (Deut. 34:7); but it was not God's will, and that is the only will that matters.

Moses was not allowed to enter the Promised Land, but he was permitted to see it. He was also given divine assurance that the land he saw was the very land God had promised to give to the patriarchs. God did not promise Moses that the Israelites would get safely across the Jordan or that they would defeat the Canaanites. God assured Moses that he brought them to the right place. Someone else would take over from there. God's faithful servant had to learn to die by faith, just as he had lived by faith. He had done well, but he had not accomplished God's plan. Only in league with others who would come after would the work finally be completed in the person of God the Son. So it is for each of God's servants. Our time runs out before the task is completed, so we finish the work only in partnership with others and with Christ.

The Hebrew text does not specify who buried Moses, just "he" buried him (34:6). We are safe in assuming, however, it was God himself because "LORD" is the antecedent to which the pronoun points in verse 5. That would explain why no one knows where Moses is buried (v. 6). Even Moses, the most faithful of God's servants, came to a lonely end, unaccompanied even by his family. Yet he was not alone, for Yahweh himself saw him safely home.

Notes

INTRODUCTION

1. Gareth L. Cockerill, *Hebrews: A Bible Commentary for Bible Students*, Wesleyan Bible Study Commentary, rev. ed. (Indianapolis: Wesleyan Publishing House, 2012), 83.
2. Andrew Murray, *The Holiest of All: An Exposition of the Epistle to the Hebrews*, 2nd ed. (London: James Nisbet & Co., 1895), 108.
3. Cockerill, *Hebrews*, 83.
4. Murray, *Holiest of All*, 110n1.

CHAPTER 1

1. Terence E. Fretheim, *Exodus*, Interpretation: A Bible Commentary for Teaching and Preaching (Louisville: John Knox, 1991), 40.
2. John Telford, "Childhood at Epworth," in *The Life of John Wesley*," Wesley Center Online, accessed October 10, 2014, http://wesley.nnu.edu/?id=84.
3. A Methodist Preacher, "The Epworth Household," in *John Wesley, the Methodist: A Plain Account of His Life and Work* (New York: The Methodist Book Concern, 1903); Wesley Center Online, accessed October 10, 2014, http://wesley.nnu.edu/john-wesley/john-wesley-the-methodist/.
4. For additional similarities, see Victor P. Hamilton, *Exodus: An Exegetical Commentary* (Grand Rapids, MI: Baker Academic, 2011), 24–25.
5. Fretheim, *Exodus*, 44–45.

CHAPTER 2

1. Victor P. Hamilton, *Exodus: An Exegetical Commentary* (Grand Rapids, MI: Baker Academic, 2011), 43.
2. Umberto Cassuto, *A Commentary on the Book of Exodus*, trans. Israel Abrahams (Jerusalem: The Magnes Press, 1967), 31.
3. James K. Bruckner, *Exodus*, New International Biblical Commentary (Peabody, MA: Hendrickson, 2008), 39.
4. Cassuto, *Exodus*, 31.
5. J. Goldingay, as cited in Hamilton, *Exodus*, 66.
6. Thomas Aquinas, *Summa Theologica*, trans. Fathers of the English Dominican Province, vol. 3 (South Bend, IN: Christian Classics, 1948), 1203.
7. Yahweh, usually translated LORD (small capital letters in some modern translations), has long been mispronounced as Jehovah.

CHAPTER 3

1. R. Alan Cole, *Exodus: An Introduction and Commentary*, Tyndale Old Testament Commentaries (Downers Grove, IL: InterVarsity Press, 1973), 76.
2. Umberto Cassuto, *A Commentary on the Book of Exodus*, trans. Israel Abrahams (Jerusalem: The Magnes Press, 1967), 50.

CHAPTER 4

1. Miriam Lichtheim, "The Admonitions of Ipuwer," in *Ancient Egyptian Literature: A Book of Readings*, vol. 1, *The Old and Middle Kingdoms* (Berkeley: University of California Press, 2006), 151.
2. Ibid., 205; with a spelling of "Hapy."
3. Although bricks were more often baked in the sun, they were sometimes fired (see Gen 11:3).

CHAPTER 6

1. James K. Hoffmeier, *Ancient Israel in Sinai: The Evidence for the Authenticity of the Wilderness Tradition* (Oxford: Oxford University Press, 2005), 85.
2. Augustine, quoted in Philip Schaff, ed., *Nicene and Post-Nicene Fathers, First Series*, vol. 7, trans. John Gibb (Buffalo, NY: Christian Literature, 1888), accessed June 24, 2015, http://www.newadvent.org/ fathers/1701055.htm.

NOTES

CHAPTER 7

1. James K. Hoffmeier, *Ancient Israel in Sinai: The Evidence for the Authenticity of the Wilderness Tradition* (Oxford: Oxford University Press, 2005), 155; William G. Dever, *Who Were the Early Israelites and Where Did They Come From?* (Grand Rapids, MI: Eerdmans, 2003), 98.

2. Joseph Callaway, "The Settlement in Canaan," in Hershel Shanks, ed., *Ancient Israel: From Abraham to the Roman Destruction of the Temple*, rev. ed. (Upper Saddle River, NJ: Prentice-Hall, 1999), 55–89. Biblical writers sometimes use the term for *one thousand* as symbolic for a multitude, as in Exodus 1:9, 20; and Deuteronomy 1:11.

3. Hoffmeier, *Ancient Israel in Sinai*, 162.

4. Victor P. Hamilton, *Exodus: An Exegetical Commentary* (Grand Rapids, MI: Baker Academic, 2011), 255.

5. We read of a similar quail invasion in Numbers 11 but cannot be sure whether it describes this event or a different one.

6. Thomas Aquinas, *Summa Theologica*, trans. Fathers of the English Dominican Province, vol. 3 (South Bend, IN: Christian Classics, 1948), 1740.

CHAPTER 8

1. Hammurabi was the sixth ruler of Babylon's First Dynasty (1792–1750 BC). His law contains a prologue, 282 laws, and an epilogue. The eighth law of the Code of Hammurabi says, "If any one steal cattle or sheep, or an ass, or a pig or a goat, if it belong to a god or to the court, the thief shall pay thirtyfold therefore; if they belonged to a freed man of the king he shall pay tenfold; if the thief has nothing with which to pay he shall be put to death." L. W. King, trans., *The Code of Hammurabi*, 1915, public domain, accessed March 4, 2016, http://www.general-intelligence.com/library/hr.pdf.

Compare this to Exodus 22:1–4, which says, "Whoever steals an ox or a sheep and slaughters it or sells it must pay back five head of cattle for the ox and four sheep for the sheep. If a thief is caught breaking in at night and is struck a fatal blow, the defender is not guilty of bloodshed; but if it happens after sunrise, the defender is guilty of bloodshed. Anyone who steals must certainly make restitution, but if they have nothing, they must be sold to pay for their theft. If the stolen animal is found alive in their possession—whether ox or donkey or sheep—they must pay back double."

2. "Citizenship Rights and Responsibilities," US Citizenship and Immigration Services, US Department of Homeland Security, accessed June 12, 2015, http://www.uscis.gov/citizenship/learners/ citizenship-rights-and-responsibilities.

CHAPTER 9

1. The Hebrew word could be translated in the singular (god) or plural (gods). The singular is more likely correct because Aaron made only one calf, not two.

CHAPTER 10

1. Gordon J. Wenham, *Numbers: An Introduction and Commentary*, Tyndale Old Testament Commentaries (Downers Grove, IL: InterVarsity Press, 1981), 110.
2. William L. Moran, ed. and trans., *The Amarna Letters* (Baltimore: Johns Hopkins University Press, 1992), 240, 249.

CHAPTER 11

1. Based loosely on Bill T. Arnold and Bryan E. Beyer, *Encountering the Old Testament: A Christian Survey* (Grand Rapids, MI: Baker, 1999), 147.
2. A. Baird and S. Samson, "Music Evoked Autobiographical Memory after Severe Acquired Brain Injury: Preliminary Findings from a Case Series," *Neuropsychological Rehabilitation: An International Journal* 24, no. 1 (2014): 125–143; Karen Ludke, Fernanda Ferreira, and Katie Overy, "Singing Can Facilitate Foreign Language Learning," *Memory and Cognition* 41, no. 1 (January 2014): 41–52; Vinoo Alluri et al., "From Vivaldi to Beatles and Back: Predicting Lateralized Brain Responses to Music," *NeuroImage* 83 (December 2013): 627–636.

Life Lessons from the Patriarchs

 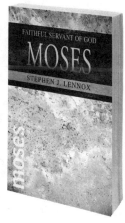 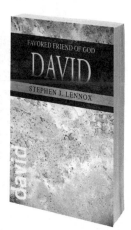

Bible scholar Stephen J. Lennox transports you back in time, immerses you in the world of the ancients, helps you unravel the significance of this giant of the faith, and provides life reflections that help you connect the truth of Scripture with modern life, discipleship, and ministry. Let Lennox serve as your competent and faithful guide as you discover what God called Abraham, Moses, and David to be and do and what difference it all makes in your life.

Abraham:
Father of All Who Believe
978-0-89827-904-7
978-0-89827-905-4 (e-book)

Moses:
Faithful Servant of God
978-0-89827-906-1
978-0-89827-907-8 (e-book)

David:
Favored Friend of God
978-0-89827-908-5
978-0-89827-909-2 (e-book)

1.800.493.7539   wphstore.com